THE
REAL ESTATE
SECRET

HOW TO MAKE A FORTUNE
WITHOUT EVER BUYING, SELLING,
OR INVESTING IN PROPERTY

Limitations Regarding Intended Use

The materials provided and prepared by Russ Dalbey are for general educational and informational purposes only and are not intended to constitute, and should not be deemed to be, financial or legal advice or an offer to buy or sell or a solicitation of an offer to buy or sell securities. Such materials do not constitute an endorsement or recommendation of any security or investment. Further, the opinions expressed herein are those of Russ Dalbey based on his experience and the experience of his top students. Under state or federal law, secured seller financed promissory notes may be considered securities, which are subject to broad regulation. These laws may require that persons who offer or sell such notes to file a registration statement with one or more regulators or rely on a legal exemption, which may or may not be available. State and federal law also may require persons regularly engaging in securities transactions to register or become licensed as securities brokers or investment advisers. Persons wishing to follow Russ Dalbey's training should consult with a qualified attorney about obligations they may have under federal, state or local laws regarding securities compliance, and business, real estate broker, and mortgage broker licensing.

Russ Dalbey
2525 Arapahoe Ave
Suite E-212
Boulder, CO 80302

Copyright © 2009, IPME, LLLP

Published By Successful Living, Inc.

Edited by Andrew Steiner, April DeMinco, and Drew Nienaber
Designed by Ryan Davis

Manufactured in the United States of America

Dalbey, Russ
    The Real Estate Secret / Russ Dalbey
    Includes Index
    ISBN 978-0-9815108-2-8

*Dedicated to all Americans that have struggled
financially like I have. Thank goodness that I met a man
that cared enough that shared the secrets that I will reveal to you.
Using these secrets you too could end your financial struggles.*

-Russ Dalbey

"Well one of the things that I really liked about the business was the fact that you didn't have to invest a small fortune to get going in it to make money! I have made $9,459.00."

- Student, Lewis D., Texas

"I have been a single mother. I have struggled for eleven years, and I now see a light at the end of the tunnel. Because of this information, I'm now able to make the kind of money that I need to make to get out of debt, and have fun with my family. I have made $40,665.00."

- Student, Eden A., Oklahoma

"This business is so easy and so lucrative that anyone can do it... This information is going to facilitate me in being able to quit the 9 to 5 grind, and be able to work my own hours, in my own way, and to make more money in less time! I have made $4,369.00."

- Student, Curtis Z., California

"Just follow Russ, he lays it out for you in this book... anybody can do it... just be persistent and keep at it... For me it's meant financial freedom! I have made $4,500.00."

- Student, Phillip D., Texas

The money making success stories listed above (and throughout this book) have all followed the information you are about to read, applied it, worked at it and made money. Keep in mind thousands and thousands of people have bought my system and most of them never report back to me. So I have no way of knowing the true average of "everyone." But I know for a fact, of the money making students who actually get back to me, the average is $3,600 per closed real estate IOU/note transaction. See page 196 to read about hundreds of additional money making success stories.

Table of Contents

Table of Contents

CHAPTER 3
Exploring Your Role as a Note Finder   67

CHAPTER 4
Insider Secrets   83

CHAPTER 5
Getting Results and Making Money   109

Table of Contents

Table of Contents

About the Author

> *"Personal success certainly offers material satisfaction. But the real joy of success comes from using your experience to elevate the lives of others."*
>
> - Russ Dalbey

ABOUT THE AUTHOR

As the CEO and founder of Dalbey Education, Russ Dalbey has authored dozens of articles on the seller financed real estate note business. A highly sought-after public speaker on the topics of wealth, success, and personal motivation, he is also an accomplished world-class cyclist who held the world record for the fastest one-mile for more than four years.

Russ Dalbey is a self-made, self-educated multi-millionaire who made a fortune using the same principles taught at Dalbey Education. Perhaps more than any other educator, Russ understands the importance of simplifying education so that anyone can learn it and actually use it to make money.

"Wealth isn't just for a certain privileged few," he says. "In spite of what most financial experts teach, you don't need to have money to make money. Anyone can learn to master the steps to financial freedom."

Although today Russ is considered the premier authority on making money with real estate IOUs, he wasn't always a financial success. He was once just a young kid on a bike with a dream of training for the U.S. Olympics.

Against all odds, he won international honors as a competitive cyclist, and broke the world record when he blazed through a one-mile course faster than any man before him.

But when the time came for Russ to leave cycling behind and earn a living outside of professional sports, he had nothing more than his own determination to rely on. With no college degree or job skills, he went in search of the best way to make money. Russ quickly began to learn the financial industry as a stockbroker. He was successful, but the work environment left much to be desired. When a friend happened to mention "The Real Estate Secret" to him, Russ was intrigued.

Russ left the high stress world of Wall Street behind and devoted his energy to making money in real estate without ever buying or selling property. He found a mentor to coach him and saw results immediately.

Shortly after, his personal mentor, Carl, passed away. The Executor of Carl's estate requested that Russ take over his education company. Out of deep gratitude for the man who helped him make a fortune, Russ agreed to step in as a service project – not being paid for his services. He soon discovered that helping others to achieve financial freedom was more rewarding and exhilarating than anything he had done before. While his teaching career began simply as a personal service project, Russ Dalbey decided to dedicate his life to helping as many people as possible achieve financial freedom.

Russ has been teaching his money making method now for almost two decades, and is considered among the leading educators and experts in the real estate field today. He is truly delighted to bring his vision, experience, knowledge, and energy to anyone who is just discovering real estate IOUs for the first time and anyone who is looking for a better way to live and love life.

Introduction

INTRODUCTION

Real Estate. Those two simple words hold so much power, don't they?

Working with real estate has been an avenue for achieving great wealth since the dawn of civilization. The people who own land and property have always been at the top of the food chain – for good reason. Real estate is the one universal commodity that consistently holds its value over time… or appreciates rapidly.

And in the United States, people like David Rockefeller and Donald Trump have established empires of enormous wealth by taking advantage of the basic principles of real estate investing.

You probably even know of plenty of people where you live who have become millionaires in the real estate industry. And take a closer look at all of the residential and commercial real estate "for sale" signs in your home town. Notice how a lot of them all are owned by – or offered by – the same individuals or companies? That's a sure sign that SOMEONE has made it big working with real estate.

You might be thinking to yourself, "If only I could get in on all that money."

Well, guess what: YOU CAN.

I'm absolutely serious. It doesn't matter who you are, your current financial status, or your educational background. You won't need a million-dollar nest egg to start cashing in on the profit opportunities in real estate. You don't even need to go to school or get a real estate agent's license!

I've discovered a surprising way to make money in real estate without ever buying, selling, or investing in property called – The Real Estate Secret.

When it comes to real estate, we all know one person sells, another person buys, and the banks provide mortgages, pretty simple – right?

Well, there's another part to real estate most people don't know about. It's the easiest part because you never risk one red cent buying, investing in, fixing up, or "flipping" property. And since you don't invest or buy property it's impossible for you to lose money in real estate.

Let others buy and sell property and take all the risk. By becoming a finder of these deals you can profit anywhere from a few hundred dollars to tens of thousands of dollars on every completed transaction.

Thousands and thousands of people have purchased this information and with just the few hundred that have followed the steps, made money, and reported their verified success to me have averaged $3,600.00 on every transaction. Without buying, investing, or shelling out one penny on property. It really is RISK-FREE Real Estate. And these same students have gone on to make MILLIONS and MILLIONS of dollars combined.

I know it sounds incredible – but I'm going to explain it all to you right here. It's the incredible insider world of real estate IOUs. The real estate market is in a slump right now – home prices are down... foreclosures are rising... and home buyers and sellers are stuck in the middle. On top of that, banks have made it so tough to qualify for a mortgage, even home buyers with the best credit can't get a loan.

So what does a home seller do when the banks have practically stopped giving out mortgages? Simple, the home seller becomes the bank and allows the buyer to pay for the home over time. Home sellers are turning to the tried and true strategy of "Seller Financing" to sell their homes.

In other words, the seller of a home finances the buyer of the home. The seller doesn't really loan the buyer the money but they do allow the buyer to pay for the home over time. A contract is created where the home seller receives monthly payments directly from the home buyer until the home is paid off. Officially, this contract is called a Seller Financed Real Estate Note or a Promissory Note. But it's nothing more than a fancy IOU and there are lots and lots of these IOUs out there.

The $147 billion dollar real estate "underground"

Right now there are over $147 BILLION DOLLARS worth of seller financed IOUs. And every week, millions and millions of dollars of new IOUs are created. What the banks and real estate professionals won't tell you is every IOU gives you an opportunity to make money even though you're not buying or selling a home. And you never invest one cent in real estate. You don't even buy or sell the IOUs. You simply find them.

This money making opportunity exists because most home sellers don't want monthly payments, they want cash now.

For the home seller, there's one weakness to these IOUs. Can you guess what it is? Most home sellers who sell homes with an IOU eventually get tired of receiving tiny amounts of monthly cash over time. They prefer one big lump sum cash payment.

Put yourself in a home seller's shoes. If you sold your home for $200,000, would you rather get $200,000 in cash or get paid $1,200 a month for 360 months? You'd choose cash up front – right? And so would most home sellers. And that's why many who've sold their homes with an IOU eventually prefer to turn around and sell the IOU for cash. Yup! Real estate IOUs can be sold for cash.

Now listen, I've held back one very important detail about these IOUs...

When creating an IOU, there's one big plus in the home seller's favor – charging a high interest rate. Some IOUs have interest rates of 10% and higher – nearly double the rate on most mortgages. I've even seen IOUs return as high as 12% interest and I expect them to go higher.

Let me ask you in today's economy, where else can you get a 12% return on your money? This is why wealthy buyers purchase IOUs from those who have them.

The banks once dominated the IOU market

Back in the day, banks bought IOUs directly from individuals – bank executives were investing in seller financed IOUs. So while the bank paid guys like you and me a lousy 2% or 3% interest on our money they were raking in 12% or more on their money from the IOUs. This was the banking industry's secret cash cow – a way to make money in real estate hand-over-fist without buying or selling real estate. But, they screwed it all up...

This $147 Billion Dollar private IOU market added millions of dollars to the banks bottom lines, but it was still seen by them as the "Ugly Duckling" of the banking world. Banks thought it was "beneath" them to buy IOUs directly from the "common man". So over time, they abandoned the $147 Billion Dollar IOU market in favor of what they thought were greener pastures.

Today we know the banks greed blew up in their face. But it doesn't change the fact that the banks opened a "back door" for regular folks like us.

There's a saying..."One man's trash is another man's treasure."

Well, in this case, the banks "trash" is worth billions of dollars, just waiting to be pocketed by regular folks like you and I. When the banks stopped buying IOUs, home sellers had no one to sell their IOUs to. That is until savvy, wealthy buyers, started buying IOUs directly from home sellers. It gave them a place to park their money and earn insanely high returns. I'm one of these buyers. I've bought over $1,000,000 (One Million Dollars) worth of seller financed IOUs. These IOUs earn me higher interest rates than any bank.

And for me, they have been much, much safer than investing in the stock market, especially nowadays. Don't get ahead of me... you don't have to buy or sell IOUs. You just have to find them. That's it! The buying and selling of seller financed IOUs is like a secret auction few know about.

Wealthy buyers look for the best IOUs and try to outbid each other. And fierce bidding takes place every day for the best IOUs.

Here's how YOU can make money (without buying, selling, or investing one cent in property or IOUs)

Home sellers want to sell these IOUs and wealthy buyers want to buy them. And every time one of these IOUs is bought and sold, three people can make money on the transaction...

1.   The seller (gets cash for his IOU)

2.   The buyer (gets an insanely high interest rate on the IOU and has a potentially great long-term investment)

3.   The middle man (gets a finder's fee for introducing the IOU seller and the IOU buyer)

Now, of the three, which do you think is the easiest, most hassle-free and risk-free way to make money? The middle man of course! And unlike the seller and buyer whose bank rolls limit how many times they can buy and sell, the middle man can do as many deals as he has time for because the only thing the middle man risks is time.

Without a middle man, many of these deals would never get done.

Now, the first question running through your head is probably..."Why don't buyers find these deals themselves?" Good question. Keep in mind these buyers are high wealth individuals. Quite honestly, they have better things to do with their time than look for these IOUs. They often have personal shoppers, personal chefs and personal assistants to do everything for them. These wealthy buyers rely on middle men to bring them these deals. And they reward the middle men with a piece of the action for every deal they close. It's your finder's fee.

And that's why I'm exposing The Real Estate Secret, so you can get in the middle of all this action as a "middle man" and get a healthy cut when a buyer purchases an IOU. How healthy of a cut? Well, as I've mentioned with just the few hundred middle men who I've trained and have gone out, followed my directions, made money and reported back to me – they have averaged $3,600.00 for every deal they've done.

The middle man's role is important to both the IOU seller and the buyer.

And a middle man's fee can be as low as $100 or as high as tens of thousands of dollars per deal. It all depends how big the IOU is. I've seen some top student's finder's fees as high as $51,000.00 and $79,000.00. In fact, I can tell you of all the people I've shown this to, the few hundred of those who've reported back to me have made MILLIONS and MILLIONS of dollars combined!

Obviously, I have no idea how well those who have not reported back to me have done. My gut feeling is, most of them have made nothing because they haven't actually gone out and tried it. This book is probably somewhere on their bookshelf, gathering dust.

I call the middle man's finder's fee "easy money" because you don't do any back breaking work and all told you can put in anywhere from a few hours to 40 hours working on a deal. And you can do it almost exclusively on the phone or on your computer.

To be an IOU middle man...

- You don't need any previous business experience or any special education (other than what I show you).

- You don't need any special research skills – all the information you need is publicly available and I'll show you how to find it without ever leaving your home.

- You don't need to know any wealthy buyers, you can refer your deals to my group of buyers. But, I'll also show you how to find more buyers on your own, so you can have even more buyers bidding on your deals.

- You never worry about real estate prices or buying low and selling high (you never buy or sell anything).

- You never invest money in real estate (you never even deal with a real estate agent, mortgage banker, or escrow company).

- You can start on a shoestring budget and do it in your spare time or full time. All you need to start is a phone and/or Internet connection.

- You can do the deals without ever leaving your home (You don't need to step foot on a property).

- And the most amazing thing is, it works just as well when home prices are in the dumpster as when real estate is sky high... because people are always buying and selling real estate.

And I predict real estate IOUs will EXPLODE in 2010 and for several years beyond because soon more people than ever may be forced to buy and sell homes using seller financing.

The worse the economy gets... The more you could make.

At last look, there were over $147,000,000,000 (ONE HUNDRED FORTY-SEVEN BILLION DOLLARS) worth of seller financed notes or IOUs in the United States – this is reported by the Federal Reserve. That averages to about $47,000,000 per county (Forty-Seven Million)! So, in just your county and the three counties next to you, you may be looking at upwards of close to $200 MILLION DOLLARS of seller financing deals available to you.

And every day more and more home sellers are offering to sell their homes through these IOUs – so the market gets an influx of new IOUs you can profit from. And every real estate expert and authority I've talked to confirms, the worse the economy gets and the harder it is to sell homes, the more IOUs will be created.

And one of the most successful real estate buyers of all time agrees. Donald Trump recently appeared on the Larry King show on CNN and told everyone to use seller financing (IOUs) to buy and sell homes:

> *"...as far as financing is concerned, the only financing you should be thinking about is seller financing (IOUs). If the seller won't give you financing, don't do it, because the banks are not doing their job. They're not providing financing for deals."*
> - Donald Trump, Larry King Show, CNN April 16, 2009.

Real Estate IOUs are all around you. You just find them like I'll show you and submit the information on a nationwide buyers network and collect your finder's fee when the deal closes.

Finding IOUs is easy and you'll have the opportunity to earn between $100.00 and $50,000.00 or more on every deal you close. Becoming a middle man and collecting your finder's fee doesn't require any fancy training or unique skills. If you have a phone or Internet connection, you have everything you need to succeed.

All the information on who sold their homes through seller financing is publicly available. You can find it at your local courthouse. Or you can research it on the Internet, free. I'll show you exactly where to go and what to look for. I'll take all the guesswork out.

And to make this even easier for you, I'll give you the simple one-page worksheet you need to collect your information. And when I say "simple worksheet," I mean it! It's simpler than filling out the paperwork at your doctor's office the first time you go.

Simply call or email someone who has an IOU, ask them a few simple questions, and then I'll show you where to send your information. I even provide you access to buyers who are already lined-up waiting to bid and purchase what you find.

With this book, I also give you the website where you can contact these buyers and have them bid on every IOU you find. I screen each note buyer to make sure they are serious and qualified buyers. Only then do I provide them with access to my Note Service.

And, we only let them stay on this exclusive list if they are and remain active buyers – helping you transact deals. These note buyers are instantly notified about your note the moment you list it. Then you just sit back and wait for the bids to come in.

Everyone wins! You don't need to know any IOU buyers because I'll supply them to you. But you aren't limited to just the buyers I introduce you to. You're always free to offer all the IOUs you find to any buyer anywhere. But I think you'll appreciate that I'm plugging you into a network of proven IOU buyers. It'll make your job even easier especially when starting out.

This book will reveal everything you need to find and refer real estate IOUs. You'll learn:

- How to find the list of people who have sold their homes with real estate IOUs (you'll find names, addresses and even phone numbers).

- How to tap into an exclusive group of buyers who have cash to pay for IOUs.

- How to have IOU holders find you (your phone could ring off the hook with sellers anxious for you to help them).

- How to determine how much money you should receive on each deal (I recommend you make between $2,000.00 and $5,000.00 for every deal you put together... but it's possible for you to make much more).

- And you'll get the simple one-page form to fill out for every IOU you find. That's the form you'll send to the IOU buyers so they can bid on your IOU.

I know I've thrown a lot at you and you probably have few questions. Odds are, you'll find your answer here:

Q: Is this legitimate? Why haven't I heard about this before?

A: YES it's legitimate! I've been teaching this for over 15 years. The banks used to do it. Smart buyers have been buying these IOUs for years. You haven't heard of it before because so few people do it. Many people know about seller financing and buy and sell homes through IOUs. I figured out that the middle man can be an important part of each transaction. And because banks have made it so difficult to get a mortgage, seller financing will become more popular for home sellers who want to sell a home quick. So I see this field exploding and this is your opportunity to get in and ride the wave of success.

Q: Explain again what these IOUs are:

A: It's simple. Seller financed IOUs are just like any other IOU. Think of it this way, let's say you are selling your car to your neighbor for ten thousand dollars. Of course, your neighbor doesn't have ten thousand dollars just sitting in the bank – he only has two thousand dollars available. So your neighbor asks if he can give you two thousand dollars up front and pay the remaining $8,000 over time. Your neighbor is asking to create an IOU for the $8,000. And because you deem your neighbor credible, you accept the offer, create an IOU, and give him the keys to the car. Now, each month, you receive a monthly payment from your neighbor until the $8,000 is paid off.

Real Estate IOUs are created in a similar manner. A buyer interested in purchasing a home can't seem to get the financing from a bank. So the potential home buyer approaches the home seller and asks if to pay for the home over time. If the home seller accepts the offer, an IOU is created and the seller gives the buyer the keys to the house. The home buyer now makes regular monthly payments to the home seller until the IOU is paid off.

Q: Why would a home seller who has an IOU want to sell it:

A: Simple. With an IOU, the home seller gets small monthly payments over 10, 20 or even 30 years. But, many IOU owners prefer a lump sum of cash. Here's a simple example: If I offered you $100 but told you I'd pay you $10 a month for ten months or if I offered you $60 cash right now, which would you take? Most people would take the cash right now. Even though $60 is less than $100, the fact that you get a large sum of cash all at once immediately appeals to most people. So if a home seller has an IOU, he is likely to sell it for cash, even if a buyer offers him a less than the full amount owed on the IOU.

Q: OK, so if most people who have an IOU want to sell it, why would anyone buy it?

A: GREAT QUESTION! Wealthy buyers like to buy these IOUs for two reasons.

1. These IOUs often have very high interest rates. The reason they have high interest rates is because the people who purchase a home through seller financing often do so because they don't qualify for a mortgage from a traditional bank. So this means they usually don't have perfect credit (it doesn't mean that they are bad people or not capable). The home seller who offers seller financing will put a higher interest rate on his IOU. The home buyer understands this is the best possible way to buy a home. When a buyer purchases an IOU, they get a great, higher interest rate on their investment. Everyone wins.

1. Just like my example above, wealthy buyers buy these notes for less than the total value. So in addition to getting a great interest rate, the buyer also gets a great yield on their money. It comes down to this. The owner of the IOU wants cash now instead of having the IOU as an investment. Often the IOU owner NEEDS cash quickly. The wealthy buyer sees the IOU as a long-term investment. So everyone wins. The IOU owner gets the immediate cash after selling the IOU and the buyer gets the IOU as a great long-term investment. EVERYBODY WINS. And the middle man who found the IOU and brought it to the attention of the wealthy buyer makes a finder's fee.

Q: How easy is it to find all these IOUs?

A: It's real simple. ALL the information is available for free. You can find it at your local courthouse or you can find it online. I show you exactly how to find it and where to go. If you can read, you can do this. It really is that simple to find this information.

Q: Am I limited to just the IOUs in my state?

A: ABSOLUTELY NOT! You can find IOUs all over the country from the comfort of your home. There are no geographical boundaries. It doesn't matter where you live, you can find notes anywhere. I've had students even do this while vacationing.

Q: I don't know any wealthy buyers. So even if I find a bunch of these IOUs, how will I get someone to buy them?

A: No Problem! I supply you with the web site address of a network of high-powered proven IOU buyers. Simply submit the IOUs you find to the network and wait for the bidding to begin. Buyers who are interested in your IOUs will contact you pretty quickly (sometimes within 24 hours!).

Q: How much can I make for every IOU I find and a buyer purchases? What's my true earning potential?

A: Every IOU is different. The rule of thumb is, the more money the IOU is... the more you can make. I've seen middle men make as little as $100 all the way up to tens of thousands of dollars. But here's what I know for sure. Over the years, many people have tried my system. Of the few hundred who followed my system and went out and did it and then reported back to me, the average they made per IOU deal is $3,600.00.

Now, keep in mind, thousands and thousands of people have bought this information, MOST of them never report back to me. So I have no way of knowing the true average of everyone. But I know for a fact, of the successful students who actually get back to me, the average is $3,600.00. And I truly think you too can average that if you follow the steps. In fact, I'm so positive you can get these results for yourself I even guarantee it.

You simply can't go wrong with my information because you get everything you need to jump in immediately. You don't have to figure out anything on your own. It's all laid out for you in a simple step-by-step system.

It's just 3-Simple Steps anyone can follow: Find IOUs, list them and make money when the deal is done.

Q: Our economy is struggling and real estate sales are down. Is now a good time to get started as a finder?

A: Now is the perfect time to get started. The use of IOUs is on the rise and history tells us that this trend should continue.

During the economic downturn of 1980-1981 unemployment peaked at 10.8% and inflation soared to 12.2%. You may recall that at that time, the average interest rate for a 30 year fixed mortgage hit a historical high just above 18%. And during that period, it is estimated that 40% of home sales used private IOUs – 40%... a note finder's dream.

Well, thankfully for new finders like yourself, the conditions in the current market are creating a similar spike in private real estate IOUs, a trend that should continue for years to come. In fact, I predict that in the coming years about 50% of real estate transactions will include a private IOU. Meaning the finders will have a 1 in 2 opportunity to make money with those properties that are sold.

Why? It's simple... people just can't get approved for traditional financing.

In the early 80s it was the high interest rates that were causing problems. People couldn't afford to pay 18% – imagine if your mortgage payment was approximately triple what it is right now and how difficult it would be to make those payments. So, those that wanted to purchase a home and the people looking to sell their property used an IOU to complete their real estate deals. When private IOUs are used, the seller and the buyer can negotiate the interest rate and other terms the way that work best for them.

Thankfully, high interest rates are no longer a problem. In fact, we have recently seen historically low interest rates… but the banks aren't offering financing. Potential home buyers with seemingly perfect credit are being denied bank financed loans. I even read an article about a woman, with more than $300,000 in combined annual income, tens of thousands of dollars in the bank, and credit scores that top 800, who was a denied a loan.

So if the banks aren't lending to those that seem like the perfect payor, how are people buying and selling homes?

Many will need to use private IOUs in order to buy a home. And the sellers will need you, a finder, to help them to get the cash they need.

So, read carefully and learn diligently as you get started working what I call "The Greatest Business in the World" – The Real Estate Secret.

Now, read carefully and learn diligently. I look forward to hearing your Real Estate Secret success stories as you put this dynamite information to good use.

CHAPTER 1

The Greatest Business in the World
The Basics of Seller Financed IOUs

OVERVIEW OF THIS BUSINESS

Seller financed IOUs have been in existence since the ownership of real estate. Currently there are over $147,000,000,000 ($147 Billion) in seller financed real estate IOUs nationwide.

Many people holding "notes," as IOUs are often called, would want to sell them, if only they knew the option existed. These notes or IOUs are often created in the sale of a property when the buyer doesn't have sufficient credit or cash to pay the full price or when the economy makes it difficult for people to qualify for a conventional mortgage. The seller may then take a note or an IOU, backed by a lien on the property, as part of the purchase price. Of course, this puts the seller in the position of having to manage the note, which was not what they intended when they sold the property.

For the educated seller financed note finder this creates an enormous profit potential for our lifetime, our children's lifetime and even our grandchildren's. There are so many notes in the United States alone that if you could find $1,000,000 worth of notes every day, without skipping a single day, it would take you nearly 300 years to find all of them and more are being created everyday.

You can make money with seller financed notes by doing what is known as "finding." This is when you locate someone with an IOU or a note, submit the IOU information to buyers on the Note Service, and earn a quick cash profit.

Another way is to buy notes. For a note buyer it's not uncommon to receive returns of 15% or higher. Notes can be safe for these note buyers because they are secured by property. Many insurance companies and corporate pension funds invest significant amounts of their assets in real estate notes and have done so for decades.

Until recently, only large companies, very few individuals, and some small companies have been able to participate in the seller financed real estate note business mostly due to lack of knowledge. However, this powerful information about how to work in this area is available to you in this book. If making as much money as you wish, for as long as you wish is a goal of yours, this may be the most important education you will ever receive.

THE HISTORY OF IOUs AND REAL ESTATE

The use of seller financed IOUs, or seller financed notes, has existed for thousands of years. The first records of commerce dating back to 2100 BC show the use of seller financing. Historically, in such transactions, sellers help buyers purchase property by agreeing to accept deferred installment payments for all or part of the purchase price. The property is pledged as the primary security by way of mortgages, trust deeds, land contracts, or other security agreements for the note.

Buyers for these secured, seller financed notes have always existed as well. However, until the past few decades, there was no organized method to move money from point A to point B, to create a liquid market for these seller financed IOUs, which is often referred to as a note. There were no structured channels for marketing and directing IOUs to buyers. Sellers who want, or need, to convert their notes to cash didn't have many options. What market there was for selling the paper was almost exclusively people they knew.

For decades, the most active participants in this arena were local real estate agents and brokers who purchased or created real estate IOUs, also known as real estate notes, as a method for increasing their sales transactions. As they ran out of capital, they brought in local private buyers to purchase the IOUs/notes. In the past, local banks might also be buyers.

By the mid 1950s, some private IOU/note buyers had come into existence. By the late 1970s, these techniques began showing up in some of the mainstream real estate financing literature, such as Joseph Bagby's Real Estate Financing Desk Book (Institute For Business Planning, 1977), Jack Cummings' The Complete Guide To Real Estate Finance (Prentice-Hall, 1978), and Frank Coffee's Creative Home Financing (Simon-Schuster, 1982).

The majority of the buying and selling of notes, however, was limited to the local marketplace. The further away the property was from a major metropolitan area, the less likely the chances were of finding a buyer for the IOU/note associated with that property. A huge part of this equation was the local liquidity factor. When local buyers' capital ran out, the IOUs/notes couldn't be sold in that particular locality until funds were available again.

In the case of sellers desperate for cash, this frequently led to extremely deep discounts on the sale of notes/IOUs.

By the early 1980s, individuals who had been successful at finding and/or purchasing private IOUs/notes began holding seminars and self-publishing training courses and books to draw in more potential buyers. Another objective was to create informal networks of buyers and finders – which enterprising individuals recognized would bring more liquidity to the marketplace and potentially increase the volume of deal activity.

THE POWER OF "NOTE NETWORKING"

The marketplace was dramatically altered in February of 1995, when America's Note Network (ANN), www.notenetwork.com, launched its nationwide networking system, allowing IOU/note finders to have a direct link with established buyers across the country. This significantly improved individual IOU/note finders' and buyers' ability to operate effectively on a nationwide level, subsequently generating dramatically increased exposure, understanding, and liquidity in the seller financed IOU/note industry, which ultimately contributed to a larger and more organized marketplace.

As note finder networking has grown and become more structured, more opportunities have been created for sellers, finders, and buyers to participate in more IOU/note sales. Most significantly, the increased level of transactions included more difficult and complicated deals that were previously not able to be completed.

The expansion of the seller financed real estate IOU/note industry and the increased level of transactions created a need for more educated note finders. Dalbey Education stepped up to meet this need. As Dalbey Education has grown, the finders who have gone through our rigorous training program have become more educated and efficient.

Dalbey Education has blazed the trail in unveiling the "hidden market" that previously plagued the seller financed real estate IOU/note industry while also playing a significant role in bringing a much higher degree of liquidity to the marketplace.

WHY ARE REAL ESTATE NOTES SO GREAT? BECAUSE THEY ARE SECURED!

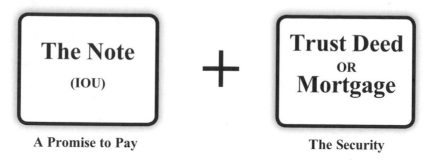

The Note

(IOU)

+

Trust Deed

OR

Mortgage

A Promise to Pay   The Security

A Real Estate Note Is A "Secured" Promise To Pay

An IOU or note states the terms in which the obligation is to be paid. These terms include the payment amount, the payment due date, the interest rate, when the note needs to be paid in full, etc. The note also contains information on who is obligated to make the payments and where those payments should be sent. The note may also contain additional terms or clauses. For example, the note may include a "due on sale" clause which states the loan must be paid off if the property is sold or transferred. We will cover some of these clauses in an upcoming chapter.

The security for these notes is provided by the pledge of the real estate. To accomplish this pledge in a legal manner, a security instrument such as a trust deed or a mortgage contract is used. These documents are similar in that they both are used to link a piece of property to a debt, but differ in how they are enforced in a foreclosure situation.

Although note holders commonly have the right to obtain legal title to the property in the event of a default, foreclosure is a legal process that involves some risk and uncertainty.

AN EXAMPLE OF HOW A SELLER FINANCED REAL ESTATE NOTE IS CREATED

Because you will be dealing with real estate notes as a note finder, let's take a minute to clarify exactly what a note is and how it is created. Let's say Bill Buyer is looking to purchase a house and he finds one that he wants to buy from Sue Seller. Sue owns her house free and clear of any mortgages or loans and her equity is $150,000. They agree on $150,000 as the purchase price. Bill has $50,000 for a down payment, but he is unable to borrow the remaining $100,000 needed from the bank.

While Sue would prefer to receive $150,000 from the sale, she needs to sell her house as quickly as possible. So they agree that Bill will make Sue monthly payments until the remaining $100,000 is paid off. Bill makes a $50,000 down payment. An IOU, or a note, is created between Bill Buyer and Sue Seller for $100,000. Sue is the note holder (mortgagee) and Bill is the payor of the note (mortgagor).

Bill agrees to pay Sue back over 30 years with 10% interest; they write all of this down as a legal agreement and sign it. This document, and the obligation to pay associated with it, is called a note.

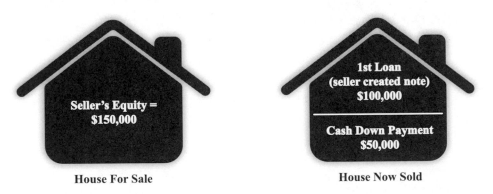

House For Sale   **House Now Sold**

The note itself is a legal contract and Bill is obligated to make the payments outlined in the agreement. But without any security for the note, Sue is limited in what she could do if Bill stops making his payments. So she asks Bill to create a mortgage. The mortgage will secure the note with the real estate that Bill just purchased from Sue. This gives Sue the right to take the house back if Bill stops making his payments. Because Sue's note was created through the sale of her real estate and it's secured by that real estate, it is also known as a seller financed real estate note. These notes are created in every county across America every day of the week. In fact, there are approximately $47 million in seller financed notes, on average, in every county across America. So, the sky is the limit for you as the note finder.

An Example of Sue Seller's Note

NOTE

December 12 , 2008   Denver_____   Colorado_____
　　　[Date]　　　　　　　　　[City]　　　　　　　　　　[State]

123 Main Street, Denver, Colorado 80211_____
　　　　　　　　[Property Address]

1.　BORROWER'S PROMISE TO PAY

In return for a loan that I have received, I promise to pay U.S. $ $100,000.00_____ (this amount is called "Principal"), plus interest, to the order of the Lender. The Lender is Sue Seller_____. I will make all payments under this Note in the form of cash, check or money order.

I understand that the Lender may transfer this Note. The Lender or anyone who takes this Note by transfer and who is entitled to receive payments under this Note is called the "Note Holder."

2.　INTEREST

Interest will be charged on unpaid principal until the full amount of Principal has been paid. I will pay interest at a yearly rate of ____10____ %.

The interest rate required by this Section 2 is the rate I will pay both before and after any default described in Section 6(B) of this Note.

3.　PAYMENTS

(A)　Time and Place of Payments

I will pay principal and interest by making a payment every month.

I will make my monthly payment on the 15th_____ day of each month beginning on January 15th_____ , 2009____. I will make these payments every month until I have paid all of the principal and interest and any other charges described below that I may owe under this Note. Each monthly payment will be applied as of its scheduled due date and will be applied to interest before Principal. If, on December 15th_____ , 2038___, I still owe amounts under this Note, I will pay those amounts in full on that date, which is called the "Maturity Date."

I will make my monthly payments at 7233 Church Ranch Blvd., Westminster, Colorado 80021_____ or at a different place if required by the Note Holder.

(B)　Amount of Monthly Payments

My monthly payment will be in the amount of U.S. $ 877.57_____.

4.　BORROWER'S RIGHT TO PREPAY

I have the right to make payments of Principal at any time before they are due. A payment of Principal only is known as a "Prepayment." When I make a Prepayment, I will tell the Note Holder in writing that I am doing so. I may not designate a payment as a Prepayment if I have not made all the monthly payments due under the Note.

I may make a full Prepayment or partial Prepayments without paying a Prepayment charge. The Note Holder will use my Prepayments to reduce the amount of Principal that I owe under this Note. However, the Note Holder may apply my Prepayment to the accrued and unpaid interest on the Prepayment amount, before applying my Prepayment to reduce the Principal amount of the Note. If I make a partial Prepayment, there will be no changes in the due date or in the amount of my monthly payment unless the Note Holder agrees in writing to those changes.

5.　LOAN CHARGES

If a law, which applies to this loan and which sets maximum loan charges, is finally interpreted so that the interest or other loan charges collected or to be collected in connection with this loan exceed the permitted limits, then: (a) any such loan charge shall be reduced by the amount necessary to reduce the charge to the permitted limit; and (b) any sums already collected from me which exceeded permitted limits will be refunded to me. The Note Holder may choose to make this refund by reducing the Principal I owe under this Note or by making a direct payment to me. If a refund reduces Principal, the reduction will be treated as a partial Prepayment.

MULTISTATE FIXED RATE NOTE

6.　BORROWER'S FAILURE TO PAY AS REQUIRED

(A)　Late Charge for Overdue Payments

If the Note Holder has not received the full amount of any monthly payment by the end of ___15___ calendar days after the date it is due, I will pay a late charge to the Note Holder. The amount of the charge will be ___15___ % of my overdue payment of principal and interest. I will pay this late charge promptly but only once on each late payment.

(B)　Default

If I do not pay the full amount of each monthly payment on the date it is due, I will be in default.

(C)　Notice of Default

If I am in default, the Note Holder may send me a written notice telling me that if I do not pay the overdue amount by a certain date, the Note Holder may require me to pay immediately the full amount of Principal which has not been paid and all the interest that I owe on that amount. That date must be at least 30 days after the date on which the notice is mailed to me or delivered by other means.

(D)　No Waiver By Note Holder

Even if, at a time when I am in default, the Note Holder does not require me to pay immediately in full as described above, the Note Holder will still have the right to do so if I am in default at a later time.

(E)　Payment of Note Holder's Costs and Expenses

If the Note Holder has required me to pay immediately in full as described above, the Note Holder will have the right to be paid back by me for all of its costs and expenses in enforcing this Note to the extent not prohibited by applicable law. Those expenses include, for example, reasonable attorneys' fees.

7.　GIVING OF NOTICES

Unless applicable law requires a different method, any notice that must be given to me under this Note will be given by delivering it or by mailing it by first class mail to me at the Property Address above or at a different address if I give the Note Holder a notice of my different address.

Any notice that must be given to the Note Holder under this Note will be given by delivering it or by mailing it by first class mail to the Note Holder at the address stated in Section 3(A) above or at a different address if I am given a notice of that different address.

8.　OBLIGATIONS OF PERSONS UNDER THIS NOTE

If more than one person signs this Note, each person is fully and personally obligated to keep all of the promises made in this Note, including the promise to pay the full amount owed. Any person who is a guarantor, surety or endorser of this Note is also obligated to do these things. Any person who takes over these obligations, including the obligations of a guarantor, surety or endorser of this Note, is also obligated to keep all of the promises made in this Note. The Note Holder may enforce its rights under this Note against each person individually or against all of us together. This means that any one of us may be required to pay all of the amounts owed under this Note.

9.　WAIVERS

I and any other person who has obligations under this Note waive the rights of Presentment and Notice of Dishonor. "Presentment" means the right to require the Note Holder to demand payment of amounts due. "Notice of Dishonor" means the right to require the Note Holder to give notice to other persons that amounts due have not been paid.

10.　UNIFORM SECURED NOTE

This Note is a uniform instrument with limited variations in some jurisdictions. In addition to the protections given to the Note Holder under this Note, a Mortgage, Deed of Trust, or Security Deed (the "Security Instrument"), dated the same date as this Note, protects the Note Holder from possible losses which might result if I do not keep the promises which I make in this Note. That Security Instrument describes how and under what conditions I may be required to make immediate payment in full of all amounts I owe under this Note. Some of those conditions are described as follows:

If all or any part of the Property or any Interest in the Property is sold or transferred (or if Borrower is not a natural person and a beneficial interest in Borrower is sold or transferred) without Lender's prior written consent, Lender may require immediate payment in full of all sums secured by this Security Instrument. However, this option shall not be exercised by Lender if such exercise is prohibited by Applicable Law.

If Lender exercises this option, Lender shall give Borrower notice of acceleration. The notice shall provide a period of not less than 30 days from the date the notice is given in accordance with Section 15 within which Borrower must pay all sums secured by this Security Instrument. If Borrower fails to pay these sums prior to the expiration of this period, Lender may invoke any remedies permitted by this Security Instrument without further notice or demand on Borrower.

WITNESS THE HAND(S) AND SEAL(S) OF THE UNDERSIGNED.

_____*Bill Buyer*_____ (Seal)
　　　　　　　　　　　　　　　　　　　　　- Borrower

_____ (Seal)
　　　　　　　　　　　　　　　　　　　　　- Borrower

QUICK CASH PROFITS!
Referring A Seller Financed Real Estate Note To A Buyer For Big Bucks

Here's an example of how finding works:

As mentioned earlier, Sue Seller wanted to receive cash from the sale of her house, but chose to create a note with Bill in order to sell her home. Fortunately for Sue, she could still get the cash she needs by selling her note to a note buyer.

Your goal as a note finder is to connect Sue with someone who wants to buy her note. The way it works is first you contact Sue and ask some questions about the note she created with Bill. Next, you analyze the note information using the proven methods I will cover later in this book. Finally, you submit the note you found on my exclusive network. Let's say a buyer offers $82,000 for Sue's note which includes remaining monthly payments. The note is sold for less than what the payor owes because money in Sue's hand is worth more than what she will get 30 years into the future. Now, you need to be paid a referral fee for connecting Sue with the buyer of her note. So you reduce the buyer's offer by $6,560, which is the amount you want to make, and offer Sue $75,440 for her note. You make a referral fee of $6,560 for simply making the connection and Sue gets the money she wanted in the first place. Everybody wins.

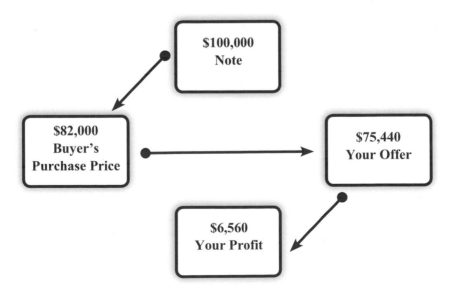

POSSIBILITIES WITH A REAL ESTATE NOTE TRANSACTION

Here's what can happen after a buyer purchases the note:

1. The payor or mortgagor (the person making the payments) makes the monthly payments, as planned, until the note is paid off. In this case the note buyer has received the anticipated return on their money.

2. The payor refinances the property and the note buyer gets paid the full amount early. Here, the note buyer receives an even greater return on their purchase because they get the full amount of the note in less time than anticipated.

3. The payments stop coming in (the payor defaults) and the note buyer forecloses, seizing all of the equity in the property. The note buyer may still profit by keeping the property and/or selling it, possibly for more than was spent! Assuming that this is a first position note and there are no other loans on this property, foreclosure can be relatively easy.

No matter what the outcome (1, 2, or 3), you, as the note finder, still profit because you get paid when the note is sold. As a seller financed note finder, you don't care what happens next with the property because you are out of the deal with no future liability.

WHY WOULD A NOTE HOLDER WANT TO SELL THEIR NOTE?

1. *Lack of confidence:*

   - In the person making the payments – the note holder is afraid that the person making the payments will stop making them or not make them in a timely manner.

- In the real estate securing the note – the note holder may fear that the property may depreciate in value, reducing the market equity that protects the value of the note.

- In the economy – the note holder may fear upcoming future economic conditions and wants a large, lump sum of cash.

2. **Deferred gratification:**

- People don't like to wait for their money.

- Give them what they want – the "now" benefit.

3. **Don't-wanters:**

- Most note holders never wanted the note in the first place (They wanted cash and this is the most common reason why note holder's sell).

- They feel as if they are stuck with the note. They would rather have the lump sum of cash now.

4. **Lack of knowledge:**

- The note holder is not aware that he/she can sell their note to a note buyer for a lump sum.

- Your new knowledge of the market will allow you to negotiate freely.

5. **Outstanding bills:**

- Note holder may need to pay for a medical emergency, taxes, pay off credit cards with high interest rates, college tuition, take a long awaited vacation – the list goes on and on. Selling the note now can provide this needed cash.

A TYPICAL REAL ESTATE NOTE

Let's take a more detailed look at another typical note, why the note holder would want to sell it, and your role in this note deal.

Here are the note details:

- Original amount of the real estate note: $30,000.00

- Interest rate: Eight percent (8%) per annum

- Term: To be paid off over 180 months (15 years)

- Monthly payment: $286.70

- Payments made: 18

- Payments remaining: 162

- Remaining balance of the note: $28,348.26

If a note buyer is looking for a twenty percent (20%) return on his/her money, the purchase price would be $16,019.92. Why would the note holder take less cash now for a $28,348.26 balance? We've already looked briefly at some of the reasons, but let's take a moment and look at more detailed reasons why the note holder would sell this note:

- **The advantage of a lump sum of cash now instead of waiting for small monthly payments.** For many people, the money due over the term of a note just isn't as satisfying as cash in hand. They want their money NOW!

- **Medical emergencies.** Unfortunate medical events can come up in anyone's life, and freeing the money tied up in the note can make dealing with these situations much easier. Money NOW will help alleviate financial stresses in an already stressful time.

- **Immediate cash to pay off tax debt.** As we all know, tax collectors want their money NOW, and the fees and penalties they extract can be painful. Selling the note will let the note holder resolve an otherwise financially painful problem.

- **Pay off credit card debt.** Credit cards charge a much higher rate of interest than is customarily put in a real estate note. This means the note holder could be paying higher interest than they are collecting.

- **Paying for college education.** When it comes time to send the kids off to college, they need money to pay tuition, room and board, and travel expenses. Money NOW will help pay for their children's education, something that will give them unlimited opportunities in life.

- **Buying a new home or business.** When a homeowner sells their home, they usually have plans to buy other property, perhaps a retirement home, or a vacation place on the shore. Having cash NOW will often help them qualify for this new loan, especially if they are retiring with reduced income.

- **Taking that dream vacation.** Having the money NOW can pay for that wonderful trip to the islands or around the world. With many of the Baby Boomers coming to retirement age and selling their homes, having money NOW will let them take the vacation they have always dreamed of and have never been able to afford.

- **Retirement.** When they retire, many people want all of their assets in what they consider very low risk or secure places, like savings accounts in banks or other low paying, but seemingly very secure accounts.

- **Divorce.** When couples split up, they often need the cash that is tied up in the note to buy new homes or settle accounts with each other, and they want to do it NOW.

- **Distribution of partnership.** Perhaps the house was owned by a partnership, and they are now parting ways. Much like a divorce, the partners want their money NOW in order to avoid complicated, drawn out payment schedules.

- **Division of inheritance.** Families often inherit real estate when parents or other relatives pass-on. To be able to divide up the proceeds, they need money NOW.

As you can see, there are a number of situations where the note holder would need your services to help them get cash now. But the most common reason is that the note holder didn't want the note in the first place, they wanted cash.

Now, how could you make money while also helping the note holder in these situations? Well, let's say that the person holding the $30,000 note, with a balance of $28,348.26, needs $13,000 cash to pay off medical expenses. You could refer the note to the buyer at a 20% yield or $16,019.92 and pocket the $3,019.92 difference! This way, the buyer gets a great return on the investment and the note holder gets cash now. Meanwhile, you get a great referral fee for bringing these two parties together! Again, it's a win-win situation for everyone.

THE PSYCHOLOGY BEHIND WANTING CASH NOW

Which would you rather have: the $50 in my left hand or the $100 in my right? That's easy! The $100, of course.

What if you had to wait seven years to collect the full $100, but you could have the $50 now? Which would you rather have? The $50, of course.

Many note holders feel the same way and want their money now! This desire compels note holders to accept a discount.

More reasons note holders want cash now:

- They have the ability to make a lot of money on other investments if their money is not tied up in a note.

- Big Dollar Amounts vs. Little Dollar Amounts – Lump Sum vs. Small Monthly Payments – Having a big lump sum of cash now is much more appealing than small monthly payments.

- Fear of Delinquent Payments – They fear that the note won't be worth anything if the payor defaults (doesn't pay).

- Relatives or Friends – Note holders will do almost anything to avoid having to foreclose on a friend or relative, and will sell at a steep discount to avoid a potential future conflict.

- Don't Know How To Foreclose – Many note holders don't understand the foreclosure process, or are reluctant to hire a real estate attorney in an attempt to recoup their loss.

- Tangible vs. Intangible Value – Note holders won't discount the house, because that's a tangible asset, but they will discount the note because it's intangible.

THE TIME VALUE OF MONEY
Why A Dollar Is Worth More Today Than Tomorrow

When determining the current value of a real estate note, many factors must be considered:

- Where is the property located?

- What type of property is it, and what are the values of similar properties in the area or community? This is commonly known as "pulling comps" on a property.

- What is the interest rate, payment amount, and original amount of the note?

- How long of a time period was given to pay off the note?

- Is there a penalty for pre-payment?

But one of the most important factors in determining the value of a note is the length of time it will take to collect all of the payments. The longer you wait, the less value or buying power that money has due to inflation and economic conditions. This is referred to as the Time Value of Money. Immediate cash is more valuable than money to be received in the future.

Time Value of Money

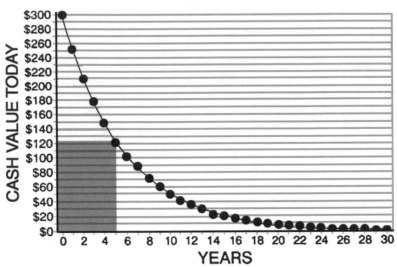

Above is a graph that gives you a general idea of how the Time Value of Money works. The graph plots the diminishing cash value of a $300 monthly payment over thirty years (a term of 360 months). As the chart shows, the cash value of the payment rapidly diminishes as it stretches into the future. For example, a note buyer looking for an eighteen (18) percent yield would only pay $123 today for a $300 payment due in five years.

A REAL ESTATE SECRET SUCCESS STORY

"This is just incredible! I get to help people and make money doing so. I've made over $64,847.02 so far!"

- Student, Chuck L., California

Creative Deal Structuring

To be a strong and educated force in the note business, it's important for you to know what a note deal looks like, from start to finish, as well as be familiar with the paperwork that will be changing hands. Although we do not recommend that you purchase notes and/or payment streams, I will walk you through one of my first note deals, from start to finish. This will help you begin to think like a note buyer, even if you're not the one doing the purchasing.

In the beginning the only way you could make money was if you purchased notes yourself and that's how I got started. It was risky because you had to put up your own money to make money. And it's important to know that I was determined to find a way that anyone who had the desire to improve their financial situation could do so without risking one dime by investing in notes and property. I've done it! Through nearly 20 years of hard work and effort I created a system so powerful that you can use it right from home in your spare time to earn unlimited income all without risking one dime buying, selling, or investing real estate.

Now you can you get involved with deals just this without having to buy or sell the note. You just connect the note holder with a seller financed note buyer and you could make a healthy referral fee.

It's simple. First, you locate a note holder that wants to sell. You collect the information the buyer will need to purchase the note and you collect your fee when the deal is complete.

To purchase a note, a note buyer will need a few documents and pieces of information. Specifically they will need:

- Copy of Note

- Copy of Trust Deed, Mortgage, or Land Contract

- Escrow instructions and closing statement from real estate sale in which the Trust Deed/Mortgage was created

- Title insurance policy which insures the Trust Deed

- Hazard insurance information on the property (Insurance Company, Policy Number, Agent's Name and Address)

- Loan Payment Record

- If available most recent appraisal and credit report

As you can see this is a lot of information to get and you may be expected to get some if not all of this information from the note holder and pass it on to the note buyer. Some buyers require more information from you while others prefer to collect the information themselves. However, all of the information listed here is the standard information required for most note purchases.

A DEAL START TO FINISH

Using one of my first deals, I will show you some of the paperwork involved in a typical transaction. This is a real life transaction, complete from start to finish. By following my transaction from start to finish, you will gain an "insider's look" at how a note deal is transacted and what documents are involved in a note sale. Copies of all documents from my first deal are available online at: **www.notefindersresourcekit.com/firstdeal**

On the next page, you will notice a copy of the note titled, "Note Secured By Deed Of Trust." Next, notice that the dollar amount in the upper left hand corner is $28,000.00; the date in which it was created: December 21, 1989; the date that it is to be paid by: December 28, 1993, four years later. "Place designated by beneficiary" is where the payments are to be sent.

A REAL ESTATE SECRET SUCCESS STORY

"When I received that bank transfer for $51,000.00 I was so excited I felt like crying!"

- Student, Kimberly M., Ohio

NOTE SECURED BY DEED OF TRUST

STRAIGHT NOTE

$ 28,000.00 ...., California .... December 21 ...., 19 89

On ..OR BEFORE:.. December 28, 1993 .... and for value received I promise to pay

to .. LONG KIM   AND TUONG VAN THI   , Husband and Wife ....

or order at .... Place designated by beneficiary .... the sum of

.... TWENTY EIGHT THOUSAND AND NO/00 ----------- .... Dollars

with interest from December 28, 1989 .. until paid, at the rate of .... 9% .... percent per annum,

payable INTEREST ONLY MONTHLY, OR MORE, in the amount of $210.00, beginning
January 28, 1990, and continuing until December 28,   1993 at which time
the remaining principal balance and accrued interest will be due and payable in
full.
Trustor herein has the option to extendthe final due date for an additional year
(1 year), and in consideration for same Trustor agrees to reduce the principal balance
of the Note by a 10% reduction.

In the event that any installment shall be overdue in excess of 15 days a late charge
of 5% of the payment due shall be charged by the holder of the note.

In the event of sale, transfer, conveyance, or alienation of the property described
in the deed of trust securing this note, or any part thereof, or any interest therein,
whether voluntary or involuntary, beneficiary shall have the right of acceleration, at
its option to declare this note, irrespective of any maturity date expressed herein,**

Should the interest not be so paid it shall thereafter bear like interest as the principal. Should default be made in payment
of any installment of interest when due, the whole sum of principal and interest shall, at the option of the holder of this Note,
become immediately due. If action be instituted to enforce payment of this Note, I promise to pay a reasonable sum as attorney's fees. Principal and interest payable in lawful money of the United States. Notwithstanding anything contained herein
to the contrary, the amount of interest payable under the terms of this Note shall in no event exceed the maximum amount
of interest permitted to be charged by law date hereof. This Note is secured by a deed of trust to South Coast Title Company,
Trustee.

**and without demand or notice immediately due and payable, including any prepayment
  charge provided for herein.

David J.

David J.

Denise R.

Denise R.

December 29, 1989, The principal balance on the within note is adjusted to
be $27,000.00, through escrow number 2-5769 WM, the payment monthly is adjusted
to be $202.50, or more.

Wanda Minini
South Coast Title Escrow by Wanda Minini

The dollar amount of the note is written out and is followed by the date in which the interest will begin – December 28, 1989. The interest rate on this note is 9% and is paid monthly in the amount of $210, from January 28, 1990 until December 28, 1993. At this time, the full principal balance and accrued interest will be due and payable in full (Later the note balance was changed to $27,000 – see clause under signatures above – and the payment reduced to $202.50 per month).

Notice that this note is not a fully amortized loan, but rather an interest-only loan. This means that the monthly payment is enough to only cover the monthly interest. You can check this by taking the original loan amount ($27,000) and multiplying it by the interest rate (9%) – you will get $2,430. That's the simple interest for a year, so dividing $2,430 by 12 will give you the monthly interest payment – $ 202.50. In this case, the monthly payments only cover the interest that is accruing, they do not reduce the principal amount owed. So you can see that this $27,000 note will still have a balance of $27,000 at the end of four years. What will the balance be at the end of three years? It would still be $27,000, right? Yes! An interest-only note will always have a balloon payment (larger payment due at a certain point in the term of the note), and that balloon payment will be the very same amount as the original amount borrowed.

This next clause is a little unusual: "Trustor herein has an option to extend the final due date for an additional year." When calculating the purchase of this note using my optimal yield, I had to expect that this clause would be exercised, and that I would have to wait an additional year to receive the balloon payment of $27,000. On the other hand, it opened the possibility that I would be able to collect an additional year of interest, so I knew that it wouldn't be a completely unfortunate situation for me if the payor should choose to extend the note term.

Another clause here is a late payment fee, which means if the payor or Trustor is more than fifteen days late, a 5% late charge would apply to their monthly payment amount. An additional clause is a "due on sale clause" – if the payor was to sell the property, prior to the notes maturity date or before the note is paid in full, the full balance of the note would be due.

The next paragraph contains some boilerplate information stating that if the payor does not pay, the Trustee, a neutral third party (in this case it is the title company), can file foreclosure.

The note is signed by the payors as they are promising to make these payments.

What did I actually get when I purchased this note? Well, it was a $27,000 note with a $202.50 monthly payment. I bought it for $14,800 and received an annual return of 41.86%.

You will notice also that this note is a straight note. This is a loan with periodic interest-only payments and then the principal sum is due in one lump sum upon maturity.

By the way, if I was to refer this note to another buyer and not purchase it myself, I could turn around and offer the note to a note buyer for a yield of 18% or approximately $22,800. I would have had an agreement with the seller for $14,800 and an agreement with the buyer for $22,800 and made a quick cash profit of $8,000.

In other words, my quick cash profit for finding the note would have been $8,000. It's the same amount of work either way. Now that's powerful!

I am providing this information because you can turn any of your transactions into bigger and more powerful profits simply by understanding some of these concepts.

THE SECURITY INSTRUMENT

Depending on what state you live in, the security instrument may be called a deed of trust, a mortgage, a land contract, a security deed, a mortgage deed, a real estate contract, or some other name. This may sound a little complicated, but really it's not. These are just different names for basically the same document.

Remember, the person who owns the note is called the Beneficiary (in a trust deed state) or the Mortgagee (in a mortgage state) – and gives their residence address or address to where any notice or payment is to be mailed. This address is where you will want to market your services to.

The security instrument has to be notarized before it is recorded. This means the borrower signs the note and security instrument in front of a notary, then the notary puts his/her seal on that document to make it official. It can now be recorded at the county recorder's office to protect the note holder's interest.

Something to keep in mind – if a buyer purchases a trust deed on a property believing that it is in the 1st position, and it turns out someone else already has a first position trust deed recorded on that same property, they may lose. They didn't check the legal records. That's why it is very important to get a preliminary title search showing existing liens and get title insurance to protect them down the road if any liens show up. I will show you more about this shortly.

Recording is very important. The mortgage is worth just about nothing until it's recorded at the country recorder's office which makes it official. And the nice part about all of this, as a note finder, is you don't have to worry about creating any of the documents because they were already created in the real estate transaction.

Generally speaking, in a note deal, the money should change hands after the recording takes place. This way the buyer knows that they have a valid lien on the property and it has been properly recorded. This is what the escrow company does to protect the buyer's interest.

Another aspect of recording is this: recorded documents are open to the public for review. You or anyone else can go to the recorder's office, register of deeds, or the courthouse to look them up yourself. This is also the main source of information for title insurance companies. They organize the data into a form that is much easier to understand and assure that the information is correct.

Title insurance insures that title to the property is clear. A note buyer will purchase title insurance to make sure they are purchasing a real recorded note secured by the property and to ensure that the property is not securing any unknown loans. And if there happens to be a mistake in the title information, the company issuing the title insurance will have to cover the note buyer's losses.

Let's take a look at the copy of the "Deed Of Trust" (the security instrument) on page 46 and I will explain some of the features. Keep in mind, if you live in a mortgage state, the security instrument is called a mortgage. Regardless of the security instrument's name, a blank copy can be obtained from a title insurance company, attorney, real estate office, or even a local stationary store.

Look at the "Deed Of Trust" (page 46) and specifically at the top left hand corner where it says, "And When Recorded Mail To." This address is the address of the note holder or the beneficiary. If a mortgage was used, this will be the address of the mortgagee – the person who sold the property and is receiving the monthly payments. At the top right, notice a stamp from the county recorders office, stating the date and time that this document was recorded. Notice the date when this document was prepared (December 21st, 1989) – it's different than the date it was recorded (January 2nd, 1990). This is normal. The date in which it is recorded is always later than the date in which the document was prepared.

Next on the "Deed Of Trust" are the names of the payors. Below that is the trustee, in this case, the name of the title insurance company. The trustee is a neutral third party such as a title insurance company or an attorney. At first, the third party's involvement in this deal may seem odd. They are not the lender, they are not the borrower, but they are named in the document anyway. That is because in the event of default on this "Deed Of Trust" the Trustee is the one who conducts the foreclosure. They are paid a fee for this. The trustee is named here and they "bear legal title." This means that they can sell the property in the event the borrower or Trustor defaults on the loan – this is the person who makes the payments and bought the property. The Trustor has the deed to the property as long as he or she fulfills the terms of the note.

Below the trustee, we see, the beneficiaries – or note holders (ones receiving the payments). And, below the note holders is a legal description of the property.

Again, as in the copy of the note, this document also mentions the "due on sale" clause. This clause is followed by the assignment of rents. This states that in the event that the Payor fails to make the payments, the note holders have the right to collect the rent (if the property is rented). In other words, when foreclosing, they can collect rent from the tenants in the property during the foreclosure process or the foreclosure period.

Next, you will notice a mention of the purpose of the trust deed, which is securing a $27,000 note.

Below the county validity section, you will see the Trustor or property owner has requested a notice of default be mailed to the included address. If the owner, or person who owes the money, defaults on the loan – this is how they are notified that they are being foreclosed on. A notice will be mailed to that address.

Finally, in the lower left is the notary information. This document is going to be signed by the Trustor (the property owner) and the notary seal is going to be placed at the bottom right of the form. In order for this document to be recorded, it must be notarized.

Additionally, there is a clause (A.1. on page 47) stating that the property owner will keep the property in good condition and repair. That means they are not going to destroy the property, tear it down, burn it down, or any other damages. Any of these would be considered in default on the agreement and have the same consequences as not making the payments. Also, there is a clause (A.2. on page 47) stating that the property owner will keep hazard insurance on the property to protect it against fire, flood, or any other local hazards. Also, we see that the Trustor, or the payor, agrees to pay the taxes and any special assessments against the property levied by governmental agencies (A.4. on page 47).

There is also a provision in the security instrument explaining what happens when the obligation is paid off. In this case, it is called "Request For Full Reconveyance." You'll see on the second page of the security instrument (on page 47) down near the bottom it says, "Request For Full Reconveyance." When the note is paid off, the "Deed Of Trust" is submitted to the trustee (the neutral third party, remember?) for full reconveyance (this removes the lien from the property).

I will also mention the foreclosure process as it relates to this "Deed Of Trust." There is a trustee named in this document, but the note holder doesn't have to use that trustee to foreclose on the note. If the note holder prefers, they could appoint someone else to take care of the foreclosure. This option is called a substitution of trustee. If for any reason the note buyer doesn't like the trustee that's named in the document, they could simply appoint another trustee instead. A real estate attorney in the area can handle this.

AND WHEN RECORDED MAIL TO

Name

Address

City
State & Zip

Long Kim
W. Balboa Bvd
Newport Beach, Ca. 92663

$5.00
C16

~10:30 AM   JAN 02 '90

Lee A. Branch RECORDER

Title Order No. _____ Escrow No. __

─── SPACE ABOVE THIS LINE FOR RECORDER'S USE ───

DEED OF TRUST AND ASSIGNMENT OF RENTS
(SHORT FORM) ADDITIONAL ADVANCE

This Deed of Trust, Made this   21   day of   December   , 19 89   , between

DAVID J.   AND DENISE R.   , herein called TRUSTOR,
Joint Tenants
whose address is   N. Adlena Dr, Fullerton, Ca. 92633
                     (Number and Street)   (City)   (State)   (Zip Code)

and SOUTH COAST TITLE COMPANY, a California Corporation, herein called TRUSTEE, and

LONG KIM   AND TUONG VAN THI   , Husband and Wife
as Joint Tenants   , herein called BENEFICIARY,

WITNESSETH: That Trustor irrevocably grants, transfers and assigns to trustee in trust, with power of sale,
that property in City of Fullerton,   Orange   County, California, described as:

Lot 16 of Tract No. 9599 as per map recorded in Book 402 pages 47 & 48 of
miscellaneous maps in the office of the County recorder of said County.

(aka: N. Adlena dr, Fullerton, Ca. 92633)

In the event of sale, transfer, conveyance, or alienation of the property described here
in, securing the note, or any part thereof, or any interest therein, whether voluntary or
involuntary, beneficiary shall have the right of acceleration, at its option to declare
the note, irrespective of any maturity date expressed herein, and without demand or
notice immediately due and payable, including any prepayment charge provided for herein.

TOGETHER WITH the rents, issues and profits thereof, SUBJECT, HOWEVER, to the right, power and authority given to and conferred
upon Beneficiary by paragraph (5) of Section A of the provisions incorporated herein by reference to collect and apply such rents, issues
and profits.
FOR THE PURPOSE OF SECURING: 1. Performance of each agreement of Trustor herein contained; 2. payment of the indebtedness
evidenced by one promissory note of even date herewith in the principal sum of $ __27,000.00_____ executed by Trustor
in favor of Beneficiary or order; 3. payment of any money that may be advanced by the Beneficiary to the then record owner of said property
with interest thereon evidenced by additional notes (indicating they are so secured) or by endorsement on the original note, executed by
the then record owner of said property.
TO PROTECT THE SECURITY OF THIS DEED OF TRUST, TRUSTOR AGREES: By the execution and delivery of this Deed of Trust and
the note secured hereby, that provisions (1) to (5), inclusive, of Section A and provisions (1) to (9), inclusive, of Section B of the fictitious
deed of trust recorded in the office of the county recorder of the county where said property is located, noted below opposite the name
of such county, vis:

County	Date	File Number	County	Date	File Number
Los Angeles	April 21, 1989	89-626684	San Bernardino	April 19, 1989	89-139423
Orange	April 18, 1989	89-202777	San Diego	February 1, 1989	89-055616
Riverside	April 20, 1989	89-125037			

(which provisions, identical in all counties, are printed on the reverse hereof) hereby are adopted and incorporated herein and made a part
hereof as fully as though set forth herein at length; that he will observe and perform said provisions; and that the references to property,
obligations, and parties in said provisions shall be construed to refer to the property, obligations, and parties set forth in this Deed of Trust.

THE UNDERSIGNED TRUSTOR requests that a copy of any notice to default and of any notice of sale hereunder be mailed to him
at his address hereinbefore set forth.

STATE OF CALIFORNIA
COUNTY OF ___Orange___   } SS.
On _December 21, 1989_____ before me, the
undersigned, a Notary Public in and for said County and State,
personally appeared _David J._____ and _____
_Denise R._____

_____, personally known to me
(or proved to me on the basis of satisfactory evidence) to be the
personS_____ whose nameS _are_ subscribed to the within
instrument, and acknowledged that ____they____
executed the same.

Signature *Pat Whisnant*
Pat Whisnant

David J. _____
David J.

Denise R. _____
Denise R.

This document filed for recording by
South Coast Title Company, Inc.,
as an accommodation only. It has not
been examined as to its execution or
as to its effect on the title.

OFFICIAL SEAL
PAT WHISNANT
NOTARY PUBLIC—CALIFORNIA
ORANGE COUNTY
My Comm. Exp. Sept. 21, 1990

(THIS AREA FOR OFFICIAL SEAL)

SC-358

SOUTH COAST
TITLE COMPANY

DO NOT RECORD—Provisions incorporated from Recorded Fictitious Deed of Trust.

A. TO PROTECT THE SECURITY OF THIS DEED OF TRUST, TRUSTOR AGREES:

1. To keep said property in good condition and repair; not to remove or demolish any building thereon; to complete or restore promptly and in good workmanlike manner, any building which may be constructed, damaged or destroyed thereon, and to pay when due, all claims for labor performed and materials furnished therefor; to comply with all laws affecting said property or requiring any alterations or improvements to be made thereon; not to commit or permit waste thereof; not to commit, suffer or permit any act upon said property in violation of law; to cultivate, irrigate, fertilize, fumigate, prune and to do all other acts which from the character or use of said property may be reasonably necessary, the specific enumerations herein not excluding the general.

2. To provide, maintain and deliver to Beneficiary fire insurance satisfactory to and with loss payable to Beneficiary, the amount collected under any fire or other insurance policy may be applied by Beneficiary upon any indebtedness secured hereby, and in such order as Beneficiary may determine, or at option of Beneficiary, the entire amount so collected, or any part thereof, may be released to Trustor. Such application or release shall not cure or waive any default or notice of default hereunder, or invalidate any act done pursuant to such notice.

3. To appear in and defend any action or proceeding purporting to affect the security hereof, or the rights or powers of Beneficiary or Trustee; and to pay all costs and expenses, including costs of evidence of title and attorney's fees in a reasonable sum, in any such action or proceeding in which Beneficiary or Trustee may appear, and in any suit brought by Beneficiary to foreclose this Deed.

4. To Pay: At least ten days before delinquency all taxes and assessments affecting said property, including assessments on appurtenant water stock; when due, all encumbrances, charges and liens, with interest on said property or any part thereof, which appear to be prior or superior hereto; all costs, fees and expenses of this Trust.

Should Trustor fail to make any payment or to do any act as herein provided, then Beneficiary or Trustee, but without obligation so to do and without notice to or demand upon Trustor and without releasing Trustor from any obligation hereof, may make or do the same in such manner and to such extent as either may deem necessary to protect the security hereof, Beneficiary or Trustee being authorized to enter upon said property for such purposes, appear in and defend any action or proceeding purporting to affect the security hereof or the rights or powers of Beneficiary or Trustee; pay, purchase, contest or compromise any encumbrances, charge or lien which in the judgment of either appears to be prior or superior hereto; and, in exercising any such powers pay necessary expenses, employ counsel and pay his reasonable fees.

5. That Beneficiary shall be entitled at any time, at its option, either by itself or by a receiver, to be appointed by a court therefore, to enter upon and take possession of said premises, or any part thereof, and to do and perform such acts of repair, cultivation or protection as may be necessary or proper to conserve the value therefor, to rent or lease the same or any part thereof for such rental, term and upon such condition as its judgment may dictate, and to collect and receive for rents, issues, and profits thereof, which said rents, issues and profits, present and future, are hereby assigned to the Beneficiary as further security, but which assignment Beneficiary agrees not to enforce so long as Trustor is not in default hereunder, and the Beneficiary shall apply such rents, issues and profits thereof, in the manner hereinafter specified in respect of proceeds of sale of said premises. In the event that the Beneficiary shall exercise the option hereby granted, Trustor agrees to surrender to the Beneficiary peaceable possession of said premises and not to interfere in any manner with the exercise of the rights hereby granted; and the expenses therein incurred, including compensation to said Beneficiary and receiver, and attorney's fees and costs and disbursements shall be deemed to be a portion of the expense of this Trust, and secured hereby and Trustor agrees to pay immediately and without demand, all sums so expended by Beneficiary or Trustee, with interest from date of expenditure at the legal rate of interest.

B. IT IS MUTUALLY AGREED THAT:

1. Should the property hereinbefore set forth ever become subject to any lien for the purpose of securing the payment of any taxes levied upon personal property of any kind or character other than household goods and furniture located in/or situated on said real property above described, then the Beneficiary shall have, and is hereby given the right, at his option, to declare all sums secured hereby immediately due and payable.

2. Any award of damages in connection with any condemnation for public use of or injury to said property or any part thereof is hereby assigned, and shall be paid to Beneficiary who may apply or release such moneys received by him in the same manner and with the same effect as above provided for disposition of proceeds of fire or other insurance.

3. By accepting payment of any sum secured hereby after its due date, Beneficiary does not waive his right either to require prompt payment when due of all other sums so secured or to declare default for failure so to pay.

4. At any time, or from time to time, without liability therefor, and without notice upon written request of Beneficiary and presentation of this Deed of Trust and the note or notes secured thereby for endorsement, and without affecting the personal liability of any person for payment of the indebtedness secured hereby, Trustee may reconvey any part of said property, and upon written request of Beneficiary, stating that all sums secured thereby have been paid, and upon surrender of this Deed of Trust and the note or notes secured thereby to the Trustee for cancellation and retention, and upon payment of its fees, Trustee shall reconvey without convenant or warranty, the property then held hereunder. The recitals in any such partial or full reconveyance of any matters or facts shall be conclusive proof of the truthfulness thereof. The grantee in any such reconveyance may be described as "the person or persons legally entitled thereto". Five years after-issuance of a full reconveyance, Trustee may destroy said note and this Deed of Trust, unless directed in such request to retain them.

5. Upon endorsement of this Deed of Trust and the note or notes secured thereby denoting any extension agreements; or any agreement subordinating the lien or charge of said Deed of Trust, or any agreement modifying the note or notes secured by said Deed of Trust; or the deeding of any easement on said property; or the making of any map or plot of said property; the consent and joinder of the Trustee in such subordination agreement, deed or map, shall not be required.

6. Upon default by Trustor in payment of any indebtedness secured hereby or in performance of any agreement hereunder, Beneficiary may declare all sums secured hereby immediately due and payable by delivery to Trustee of written declaration of default and demand for sale and of written notice of default and of election to cause said property to be sold, which notice Trustee shall cause to be filed for record. Beneficiary also shall deposit with Trustee this Deed of Trust, said note and all documents evidencing expenditure secured hereby. After the lapse of such time as may then be required by law following the recordation of said notice of default, and notice of sale having been given as then required by law, Trustee, without demand on Trustor, shall sell said property at the time and place fixed by it in said notice of sale, either as a whole or in separate parcels, and in such order as it may determine, at public auction to the highest bidder for cash in lawful money of the United States, payable at time of sale.

Trustee may, from time to time, postpone the sale of all, or any portion of said property by the publication, prior to the date of sale so advertised, of one notice of postponement in the same newspaper or newspapers in which the original notice of sale was published, or by one public announcement thereof at the time and place of sale so advertised or postponed. If the sale is so postponed, or is postponed in any manner, or if the sale for any reason is not held within one year from the time set for the first sale, the Trustee, at his election shall have the right to again give notice of sale as then required by law for an original sale. Trustee shall deliver to such purchaser its deed conveying the property so sold, but without any convenant or warranty, express or implied. The recitals in such deed of any matters or facts shall be conclusive proof of the truthfulness thereof. Any person, including Trustor, Trustee, or Beneficiary as herein defined, may purchase at such sale.

After deducting all costs, fees and expenses of Trustee and of this Trust, including costs of evidence of title in connection with sale, Trustee shall apply the proceeds of sale to payment of all sums expended under the terms hereof, not then repaid, with accrued interest at seven percent per annum; all other sums then secured hereby; and the remainder, if any, to the person or persons legally entitled thereto.

7. Beneficiary may from time to time, by instrument in writing, substitute a successor or successors to any Trustee named herein or acting hereunder, which instrument when executed, acknowledged and recorded in the office of the Recorder of the county or counties where said property is situated, shall be conclusive proof of proper substitution of such successor Trustee or Trustees, who shall, without conveyance from the Trustee predecessor, succeed to all its title, estate, rights, powers and duties. Said instrument must contain the name of the original Trustor, Trustee and Beneficiary hereunder, the book and page where this Deed of Trust is recorded, and the name and address of the new Trustee. If notice of default shall have been recorded, this power of substitution cannot be exercised until after the costs, fees and expenses of the then acting Trustee shall have been paid to such Trustee, who shall endorse receipt thereof upon such instrument of substitution. The procedure herein provided for substitution of Trustees shall be exclusive of all other provisions for substitution, statutory or otherwise.

8. This Deed of Trust applies to, inures to the benefit of, and binds all parties hereto, their heirs, legatees, devisees, administrators, executors, successors and assigns. The term "Beneficiary" shall mean the owner and holder, including pledgees, of the note secured hereby, whether or not named as Beneficiary herein. In this Deed of Trust, whenever the context so requires, the masculine gender includes the feminine and/or neuter, and the singular number includes the plural.

9. Trustee accepts this Trust when this Deed of Trust, duly executed and acknowledged is made a public record as provided by law. Trustee is not obligated to notify any party hereto of a pending sale under any other Deed of Trust or of any action or proceeding in which Trustor, Beneficiary or Trustee shall be a party unless brought by Trustee.

REQUEST FOR FULL RECONVEYANCE

To be used only when note has been paid.

To SOUTH COAST TITLE CO. Trustee:

Dated ____________________

The undersigned is the legal owner and holder of all indebtedness secured by the within Deed of Trust. All sums secured by said Deed of Trust have been fully paid and satisfied; and you are hereby requested and directed, on payment to you of any sums owing to you under the terms of said Deed of Trust, to cancel all evidences of indebtedness, secured by said Deed of Trust, delivered to you herewith together with the said Deed of Trust, and to reconvey without warranty, to the parties designated by the terms of said Deed of Trust, the estate now held by you under the same.

Mail Reconveyance To:

____

____

____

____

____

____

Do not lose or destroy this Deed of Trust OR THE NOTE which it secures.
Both must be delivered to the Trustee for cancellation before reconveyance will be made.

ORIGINAL ESCROW INSTRUCTIONS

Escrow instructions are created to inform the title office or the real estate attorney the details of the transaction. Typically they are created by the seller of the property initially. During the process of purchasing a note the note buyer will usually provide instructions to the title company of exactly what they want completed.

What a note buyer is looking for in the original escrow instructions is proof that there was a sale of real estate. The note buyer would check to see that the information matches that of the note and deed of trust. You can see when the note was created and all the details in the escrow instructions. The original escrow instructions from one of my first deals are on page 49.

CLOSING STATEMENT

The escrow closing statement (see page 50) is very important. It will give the note buyer a detailed analysis of how the money was spent on the real estate transaction and provides proof that the transaction took place. Usually the note buyer is looking to verify that there was a down payment on the property and that the information they received about the sale was accurate. The note buyer will have a hard time determining what's for sale and may back out of the deal if the information about the note and the sale of the property does not match the information on the closing statement.

ESCROW INSTRUCTIONS

12752 Valley View Ste S

Garden Grove, Ca. 92645

SOUTH COAST
TITLE COMPANY 714-898-1800
                213-594-4621

Page One	Paid Outside of Escrow $ _____
	Cash Through Escrow 27,400.00
Date September 26, 1989	Encumbrances of Record _____
Escrow Number 2-5402 WM	New Encumbrances 221,600.00
	" " 28,000.00
Escrow Officer Wanda	**TOTAL PURCHASE PRICE** $ 277,000.00

1. PRIOR TO October 31, 1989 Buyer will hand you or cause to be handed you
2. $ 249,000.00, of which a portion will be proceeds of a new loan more completely
3. described below and of which $1,000.00 will be handed you representing Buyer's
4. deposit of earnest money. Balance of down payment and necessary closing costs
5. to be deposited herein by the Buyer prior to close of escrow.
6.
7.
8.
9. and any additional funds and instruments necessary on Buyer's part to enable you to comply with these instructions, which you will
10. deliver, provided on or before the date set forth above, you hold the money and documents, if any, deliverable to Buyer under these
11. instructions and instruments have been filed for record entitling you to procure CLTA STANDARD COVERAGE FORM policy of title
12. insurance issued by South Coast Title   with title company
13. liability under terms of its policy, for the amount of total Purchase Price (or in the amount required by new Lender, whichever is
14. greater) on real property in the County of Orange   State of California, viz:
15. Lot 16 of Tract No. 9599 as per map recorded in Book 402 pages 47 & 48 of
16. miscellaneous maps in the office of the County Recorder of said County.
17.
18.
19. (commonly known as 827 N. Adlena Dr.   ca.
20.
21.
22.
23.
24.
25.
26.
27. Showing title vested in DAVID J.   AND DENISE R.   , Husband and Wife(More complete
28. vesting to be handed you prior to close of escrow which you are to insert on the
29. Deed of conveyance without further approval from the Seller)
30. SUBJECT TO:
31. [X] General and special taxes for ____ all _____ fiscal 19 89 19 90 and subsequent
32.   years, including reassessments if any and including any special district levies or personal property taxes, payment for which
33.   are included therein and collected therewith, and improvement bond assessments, when applicable.
34. [ ] _____
35. [X] Covenants, conditions, rights of way, easements and reservations of record.
36. The consummation of this escrow is contingent upon the Buyer obtaining and qualifying
37. fro a new first trust deed loan in the amount of $221,600.00, and subject to the
38. property appraising at the purchase price of $277,000.00. New loan to have a FIXED
39. rate of interest NOT to exceed 10.5% per annum, payable approximately $1,944.70 monthly,
40. including principal and interest, amortized over 30 years. Buyer to pay loan fee NOT
41. to exceed $3,000.00. Buyer's signature on lender loan documents shall indicate Buyer
42. approval of all terms and conditions therein and your instructions to comply therewith.
43.
44. As a portion of the purchase price herein Buyer to execute a Note and Deed of Trust,
45. in favor of the Seller as title now stands and to be recorded as a Second Trust Deed
46. against the subject property. Note to be in the amount of $28,000.00, with interest at
47. 9% per annum, all due 4 years from   of escrow.
48. Escrow holder is authorized to insert the interest on the Note to accrue from close of
49. escrow, at 9% per annum, payable $228.90 per month, or More. First payment shall be
50. 1 year from close of escrow.
51. Note to Contain: " All unpaid interest accruing for the first year shall be added to
52. the principal balance of the NOte and the interest of 9% per annum, shall be charged
53. thereon". Escrow holder is authorized to insert the first payment date on the note
54. to be 1 year from close of escrow and insert the final payment date to be 4 years from
55. close of escrow.
56. Note to also contain the following: "In the event that any installment shall become
57. overdue in excess of 10 days a late charge of 6% of the payment amount shall be charged
58. by the holder of the note thereof".
59. "Trustor on the Note reserves the prvivilege to pay in part or in whole the principal
60. balance plus any accrued interest, at any time prior to the maturity date without
    a prepayment penalty for so doing".

SC-1A (4/88)

SOUTH COAST
TITLE COMPANY

12752 VALLEY VIEW, SUITE S
GARDEN GROVE, CA 92645
(714) 898-1800 • (213) 594-4621

ESCROW NO. 2-54

• Long Kim   and
• Tuong Van

DATE OF RECORDING: Dec. 28, 19
PROPERTY ADDRESS: Adlena Drive
                        Fullerton, CA

ESCROW STATEMENT:	DEBIT	CREDIT
1 Total Consideration		277,000.00
2 First Trust Deed		
3 Second Trust Deed		
4 Deposit		
5		
6 **ADJUSTMENTS**		
7 Taxes $ 735.21 for 6 months from: 12/28 to: 12/31		12.24
8		
9 Home Warranty	295.00	
10		
11		
12		
13		
14		
15 Homeowner Association		
16		
17 **DISBURSEMENTS**		
18 Policy of Title Insurance	804.00	
19 ALTA Loan Title Insurance		
20 Title Company's Sub-escrow Fee	50.00	
21 Recording Deed	14.00	
22 Recording Trust Deed		
23 Recording Reconveyance		
24		
25 Documentary Stamps (on Deed)	304.70	
26 Trustees Reconveyance Fee		
27 County Tax Collector		
28 Tax Service		
29 Commission		
30 Termite Report and Work		
31		
32 Principal of Loan Paid to:	126,091.03	
33 Interest 31 09/DAY from: 12/1 to: 12/28 870.55	777.27	
14 Loan Prepayment Charges		
15 Loan Company - Service Charge		
16 Impound Credit		
17 Late charge 870.55 - 777.27 = 93.28 LOST 31.08?	124.36	
18 Federal Express	30.00	
19 Principal of Loan, Paid to:	46,450.00	
0 Interest from: to:	788.38	
1 Loan Company — Service Charge		
2 Forwarding fee / Statement fee	115.00	
3		
4 New Loan Origination paid to:		
5 Credit Report		
6 Appraisal Fee		
7 Impound Deposit: Taxes		
8 Hazard Insurance		
9		
0 Interest on $ from: to:		
1		
2		
3		
4		
5 **ESCROW CHARGES**		
6 Escrow Fee	565.50	
7 Loan Escrow Fee		
8 Preparing Deed	100.00	
9 Preparing Trust Deed		
0 Loan Tie-In Fee		
1 Handling demand	75.00	
2 Processing Fee:		
3 Buyers escrow fee	640.50	
4		
5 Balance	99,787.50	
6 TOTALS	277,012.24	277,012.24

(PLEASE RETAIN THIS STATEMENT FOR INCOME TAX PURPOSES)

THE PRELIMINARY TITLE POLICY REPORT

Continuing down the list of documents most buyers will need before purchasing a note, you'll see that a copy of the note seller's existing title insurance policy is required. You will see a copy of my preliminary title policy on pages 53-56.

Remember that the existing title insurance policy insures the note holder for any unforeseen issues that may prevent the note holder from having a clear right to title in a foreclosure situation. So if for some reason, the title agency missed something that would prevent the note holder from taking the property through foreclosure the title insurance company would then be liable.

What about the issues that the title company did find? Any known issues, such as an existing lien, are listed in the title policy as an "exception to the policy." These exceptions notify the note buyer of all known situations that would prevent them from having a clear right to the property. If the note holder can't foreclose because of a known exception, the title company is not responsible.

As you would expect, I would want to see the list of exceptions to the title policy. This would inform me of all known issues and any other liens on the property.

Keep in mind, that the title policy only lists the liens that were in place at the time the policy was issued. And more importantly, it doesn't give any information about (and doesn't insure against) any liens or issues that may come up after the policy was created. So a new tax lien or even a new first position note would not show up on the exception list.

In order to get the most up to date information, I would have to order a title report. A title report will give me the most up to date information on the title status of the particular property securing the note. Specifically it will tell me about any other unexpected liens, judgments, assessments, easements, and unpaid taxes against the property.

In this particular deal, the note seller did not send me a copy of this policy, but I did know that South Coast Title Company was providing the title insurance (their company name can be found at the top of the closing statement). So what I did was just go ahead and order a complete title report to get the information that was listed as exceptions to the first title policy and any new information that may have been added since the property was sold. You see, from my experience in this business, I knew that the title company would be familiar with this property/policy and have the paperwork on file. After all, they did handle the closing of the initial transaction, right? Also, I was planning on insuring the title through this same company and would need to be in touch with them at some point.

If you were the note buyer, all you would do is call up the title company and request a preliminary title report. And guess what? Many times it's free. Why? Remember, the title company wants to sell you one of their title policies. They are a great help in protecting the buyer and giving access to the information needed to make an informed decision as to whether or not the note purchase is a wise purchase.

On page 54 we see that there's some information that describes the property and the payor.

On page 55 we see some general information endorsed. At the bottom, in Schedule B "#5", we see an indebtedness of $221,000. That's the first position loan on the property. Okay, so far so good.

On page 56 on Schedule B "#6", we see the $27,000 trust deed that I purchased. If another trust deed was recorded before my $27,000 trust deed, then I would not have purchased the note because I would have been in third position. Third position can be OK if there is enough protective equity in the property, but in this case, third position would have prevented the deal.

When purchasing a note, a buyer can ask for a 104.1 endorsement policy (or a similar endorsement) to the existing policy. This can save the note buyer hundreds of dollars. A 104.1 endorsement is an assignment endorsement used to add the note buyer onto the existing title insurance coverage already in place for the note and the collateral property.

The 104.1 endorsement expands title insurance coverage to protect the new owner (Assignee) of the note. The use of this endorsement is designed to give the note buyer protection of their lien interest, without the expense of a whole new title policy issued solely for them.

S O U T H C O A S T T I T L E C O M P A N Y

888 West Santa Ana Boulevard, Suite 220
Santa Ana, California 92701
(714) 973-1441

Russell Dalbey

Issuing Policies Of
NORTHERN COUNTIES TITLE INSURANCE COMPANY

* * * PRELIMINARY REPORT * * *

Your No.:
Our No.: 80033-3

In response to the above referenced application for a policy of title
insurance, South Coast Title Company hereby reports that it is prepared to
issue, or cause to be issued, as the date hereof, a policy or policies of
Northern Counties Title Insurance Company describing the land and the
estate or interest therein hereinafter set forth, insuring against loss
which may be sustained by reason of any defect, lien or encumbrance not
shown or referred to as an exception below or not excluded from coverage
pursuant to the printed schedules, conditions and stipulations of said
policy forms.

The printed exceptions and exclusions from the coverage of said policy or
policies are set forth in Exhibit A attached. Copies of the Policy forms
should be read. They are available from the office which issued this
report.

This report (and any supplements or amendments hereto) is issued solely for
the purpose of facilitating the issuance of a policy of title insurance and
no liability is assumed hereby. If it is desired that liability be assumed
prior to the issuance of a policy of title insurance, a binder or
commitment should be requested.

Dated: December 2, 1991 at 7:30 A.M.

Marilyn Firman
Marilyn Firman, Title Officer

Order No.   80033-3
Page 2

SCHEDULE A

The estate or interest in the land described or referred to in this
schedule covered by this report is:

A Fee

Title to said estate or interest at the date hereof is vested in:

DAVID J.   and DENISE R.   , husband and wife as joint tenants

The land referred to in this report is situated in the State of California,
County of ████, and is described as follows:

Lot 16, of Tract No. 95   , in the City of ████████, as per map
recorded in book 402, page(s) 47 and 48 of Miscellaneous Maps, in the
office of the County Recorder of said County.

Except therefrom all oil, gas, minerals and other hydrocarbons, below a
depth of 500 feet, without the right of surface entry, as reserved in
instruments of records.

SCHEDULE B

At the date hereof Exceptions to coverage in addition to the printed
exceptions and exclusions contained in said policy form would be as follows:

A. General and special county and city taxes for the fiscal year 1991-92.
    Total   : $2,843.00
    First Installment   : $1,421.50 open
    Second Installment   : $1,421.50 open
    Exemption   : $7,000.00
    Code Area: 03003   Parcel No.: 281-141-01

B. The lien of Supplemental Taxes, if any, assessed pursuant to the
    provisions of Chapter 3.5, (commencing with Section 75) of the Revenue
    and Taxation code of the State of California.

1. The fact that the owners of said land have no rights of vehicular
    access to BASTANCHURY ROAD except the public right to travel on same.
    Said rights having been relinquished by the dedication provisions on
    the map of said Tract. Said land, however, abuts on a public street,
    other than the one referred to above, over which rights of vehicular
    access have not been relinquished.

2. An easement for purposes shown and incidental purposes
    Affects   :   The Northeasterly and the Southwesterly 4 feet of
                             said land
    Purpose   :   Public Utilities
    Recorded   :   In book 12280, page 525, Official Records

3. An easement for purposes shown and incidental purposes
    Affects   :   The Southeasterly 6 feet of said land
    Purpose   :   Public Utilities
    Recorded   :   In book 12328, page 1872, Official Records

    Said deed provides that no building or structure shall be placed or
    maintained on said easement.

4. An easement over that portion of said land as shown on the map of said
    tract,
    For   :   Landscaping
    Affects   :   The Northwesterly portion of said land

5. A Deed of Trust to secure an indebtedness of $221,000.00, and any other
    amounts as therein provided, recorded December 28, 1989, as Instrument
    No. 89-700921, Official Records.
    Dated   :   December 15, 1989
    Trustor   :   David J.   and Denise R.   , husband and
                             wife as joint tenants
    Trustee   :   Citicorp Savings Service corporation, a
                             California corporation
    Beneficiary   :   Citicorp Savings, a Federal Savings and Loan
                             Association

6. A Deed of Trust to secure an indebtedness of $27,000.00, and any other amounts as therein provided:

Dated	:	December 21, 1989
Trustor	:	David J. and Denise R. , husband and wife as joint tenants
Trustee	:	South Coast Title Company, a California corporation
Beneficiary	:	Long Kim and Tuong Van Thi , husband and wife as joint tenants
Recorded	:	January 2, 1990, as Instrument No. 90-000511, of Official Records.

The amounts due, terms and conditions of the indebtedness should be determined by contacting the owner of the debt.

7. The effect of documents, proceedings, liens, decrees, or other matters which do not specifically describe said land, but which, if any do exist, may affect the title or impose liens or encumbrances thereon. The name search necessary to ascertain the existence of such matters has not been completed and requires a statement of identity from all parties in order to complete this report.

NOTE: Section 12413.1, California Insurance Code, commonly known as Assembly Bill 512, became effective January 1, 1990. This legislation deals with the disbursement of funds deposited with any title entity acting in an escrow of subescrow capacity. The law requires that all funds be deposited and collected by the title entity's escrow and/or subescrow account prior to disbursement of any funds. Some methods of funding may subject funds to a holding period which must expire before any funds may be disbursed. In order to avoid any such delays, all fundings should be done through wire, transfer, certified check or checks drawn on California financial institutions.

WIRING INFORMATION

TO WIRE FUNDS TO SOUTH COAST TITLE COMPANY:

HARBOR BANK-11 Golden Shore, Long Beach, CA 90802 Fed Reserve #122234152 for further credit to HARBOR BANK-IRVINE BRANCH-9 Executive Circle, Irvine, CA for the Benefit of South Coast Title Company Trust Acct. #041-032-251

Said Seller does qualify for short term rate.

HAZARD INSURANCE

Alright, let's look at page 58 to see the Hazard Insurance Policy or the Homeowner's Policy. You will notice my company, Southwest Funding, was added to the homeowner's policy as an additional mortgagee – meaning that I was the one now owed the money and receiving the monthly payments.

Once I purchased the note, the escrow company sent a letter to the payor's insurance company adding me on to their hazard insurance policy. This policy would pay me and the other lenders in the event that covered damage happens to the property and reduces its value.

Whatever is left over will go to the owner of the property (the Trustor or payor).

This protects me in the event of a fire or other event that could destroy or devalue the property. I would get paid before the homeowner gets paid in the event of a disaster. Why? Because I am acting as the bank, and the bank always gets paid first.

REMAINING DOCUMENTS

There are three more items most seller financed note buyers will need before purchasing a note. The first is the loan payment record which shows that the note holder has received the scheduled payments. The second is a recent appraisal. This appraisal will prove the value of the property securing the note. Finally, the buyer will want to see the payor's credit report. The credit report will help prove that the payor is financially responsible.

As a note finder don't worry if you have a hard time getting all of these documents from the Information Request Form. Most note buyers will have their own appraisal done before they purchase the note. In addition, many of the note buyers you will come across will pull the credit score of the payor themselves. As you know, your goal is to get as many of the documents listed on the Information Request Form as you can and pass them on to the note buyer to facilitate the transaction. But don't let it stop you if you can't find every piece of documentation on the list.

HO 717 25   ***** MORTG*GEE 2 COPY *****   012192-3AS-019-1

20th Century Insurance Company
1 Owensmouth Avenue / Woodland Hills, California 91367
DECLARATION PAGE

AMENDED DECLARATION
EFFECTIVE DATE 01/21/92

HOMEOWNERS POLICY
WHEN ATTACHED TO THE HOMEOWNERS POLICY, THESE DECLARATIONS COMPLETE THE POLICY AND REPRESENT
THE CURRENT STATUS OF YOUR COVERAGES AND LIMITS OF LIABILTY ACCORDING TO OUR RECORDS.

REASON FOR AMENDMENT -
ADD MORTGAGEE

POLICY NUMBER	POLICY PERIOD		TERM
	12:01 A.M. STANDARD TIME		
HO 71725	FROM 12/22/91 TO 12/22/92		12 MO

NAMED INSURED AND ADDRESS	MORTGAGE SERVICE CO./MORTGAGEE (SEE REVERSE)
DAVID J	RUSS DALBEY SOUTHWEST FUNDING LN# 1933

COVERAGE IS PROVIDED WHERE A LIMIT OF LIABILITY IS SHOWN, SUBJECT TO ALL CONDITIONS OF THIS POLICY

COVERAGES AND LIMITS OF LIABILITY	SECTION I				SECTION II	
	A. DWELLING	OTHER STRUCTURES ON PREMISES	B. PERSONAL PROPERTY	C. LOSS OF USE	L. PERSONAL LIABILITY EACH OCCURENCE	M. MEDICAL PAYMENTS TO OTHERS
	$ 121,000	$ 12,100	$ 90,750	INCLUDED	$ 300,000	$ 5,000 EACH PERSON
DEDUCTIBLES	SECTION I $ 250	EARTHQUAKE N/A	IN CASE OF LOSS UNDER THIS POLICY, WE COVER ONLY THAT PART OF THE LOSS OVER THE DEDUCTIBLE STATED.			
PREMIUMS	BASIC POLICY PREMIUM $ 289.45	OPTIONAL COVERAGES $ 20.00	SCHEDULED PERSONAL PROPERTY $ .00		TOTAL PREMIUM 309.45	

```
---- FORMS, OPTIONS, AND ENDORSEMENTS ----      LOCATION OF PREMISES -
                                                SAME AS ABOVE
*** GUARANTEED REPLACEMENT COST POLICY
*** THIS POLICY DOES NOT INCLUDE
    EARTHQUAKE COVERAGE                         *** NOTICE ***
                                                THIS POLICY MEETS OR EXCEEDS
OPTION H, COMPUTERS $10000          $    20     THE COVERAGES PROVIDED BY
CALIFORNIA SURCHARGE (CIGA)         $  1.45     STANDARD HOMEOWNERS FORM HO-3.



438BFU *05/42--TCPE7  *06/89--TCPE6   12/89
```

James O. Curley
PRESIDENT   01/21/92
                             DATE

- - - - - - - - - - - - - - - - DETACH HERE - - - - - - - - - - - - - - - -

POLICY NUMBER	AMOUNT DUE
HO 7172581 2	

```
POLICY SERVICE PHONE: 818 704-3700
CLAIMS SERVICE PHONE: 714 836-8660


STATEMENT OF ACCOUNT  7172581  2
ADDITIONAL PREMIUM.... $    .00
PRIOR BALANCE......... $ 172.91
* OUTSTANDING BALANCE    172.91

PAYMENTS ARE REVISED AS FOLLOWS-
* PAYMENT DUE        $    .00
FUTURE INSTALLMENTS DUE
02/22/92 $  82.91 04/22/92 $  90.00

INCLUDES   3 PER PAYMENT SERV CHARGE
```

**** THIS IS NOT A BILL *****
ADDRESS INQUIRIES TO -
20TH CENTURY INS CO
P.O. BOX 4150
WOODLAND HILLS CA 91365

MAY 28 1992

FORM HOO-1 (5/91)

▲ RETURN THIS STUB WITH PAYMENT ▲

Knowledgeable buyers are skilled at digging up hard to find pieces of information. So in order to get your deal moving, send your buyer what you have and give them a list of what you're missing (Be sure to have a signed COMMITMENT LETTER and NON-CIRCUMVENT AGREEMENT before sending any documentation). From there many buyers will take the lead and locate the rest of the needed information.

There you have it! We have just covered all of the items required by the INFORMATION REQUEST FORM. It really is that easy. And the best part about all of this is you don't have to understand the information in this manual to make money, however, if you do understand it, you'll just make more money.

DETAILS FOR THE NOTE BUYER TO HANDLE BEFORE CLOSING

- The buyer will have a real estate attorney or title company prepare an assignment from the note seller(s) to the note buyer.

- Prepare a "Request for Special Notice of Default" in favor of note buyer's name. This will go to the first lien holder (if it is a second position note the note buyer is purchasing).

- Order endorsement to existing title insurance policy (this can save the note buyer hundreds of dollars at closing).

- Prepare a hazard insurance letter to cover note buyer in case of property damage.

- Review copies of the note, trust deed, request for special notice, property sale escrow instructions (for the original sale), escrow closing statements (for the original sale), title commitment for current title status, the loan payment record, a current appraisal, payor's credit report, and any other misc. documents.

- Mail property owner's debtor's offset statement confirming unpaid balance, interest rate, payment amount, next payment due, maturity date, taxes & insurance have been paid and that any senior liens are current.

- Mail note holder's offset statement confirming unpaid balance, interest rate, payment amount, next payment due, maturity date, taxes & insurance have been paid and that any senior liens are current.

- Prepare escrow instructions for the title company to handle details of the closing.

DETAILS FOR THE NOTE BUYER TO HANDLE AT CLOSING

- The buyer will review the original note, original trust deed, prepared assignment, and escrow closing statement for note purchase.

- Note buyer makes sure that they receive the original trust deed, original assignment, new title insurance policy, note holder's offset statements, and property owner's offset statements.

- Mail notice of loan and new payee to debtor of transfer.

- Verify that the note buyer's name is listed as the mortgagee (or loss payee) on the payor's home owner's insurance policy.

- Note buyer to ensure all items are met before the money is released in escrow.

Since we are on the topic of closing, what about closing costs? When finding and referring deals to buyers, we ask if the buyer is paying closing, right? If they aren't then we have to deduct an additional 3% for closing. Keep this in mind when calculating your offer.

BUYER PREPARED ESCROW INSTRUCTIONS

To simplify the escrow and closing process, many buyers will use the same escrow company, title company, or attorney that prepared the documents on the initial property sale. This saves them time, money, and hassle, as much of their work is already done. From there, many note buyers will write up their own escrow instructions, and send them to the escrow or title company to ensure that all of their needs are met in the closing process.

Remember, the title company or attorney that did the original escrow on the property sale should be able to do all of the following paperwork for the note buyer. Additionally, they help protect them and the seller of the note to ensure that everyone receives what's coming to them. And of course, the buyer will know about this but it helps to understand what the buyer needs to close a note deal. And although you are the note finder and not the buyer I do want you to have an idea of what the buyer does.

THE ASSIGNMENT

The assignment transfers ownership from the seller of the note to the buyer. Take a look at page 62 for the assignment of deed of trust from one of my first deals.

At the top you'll notice, "And When Recorded Mail To" – this is where the address of the person purchasing the note will go. Further below it states, "For value received the undersigned..." This refers to the seller of the note and grants a transfer to Southwest Funding, my company.

Next is the information about the original trustee and the property address. Lastly, it must be signed by the note seller, notarized, and recorded at the county courthouse. Once recorded, it takes about 2 to 4 weeks before the buyer will receive it back in the mail. Some counties are faster than others.

RECORDING REQUESTED BY

AND WHEN RECORDED MAIL TO
#1933

Name   Southwest Funding

Street
Address

City &
State

────SPACE ABOVE THIS LINE FOR RECORDER'S USE────

CAT. NO. NN00610
TO 1936 CA (2—83)

Assignment of Deed of Trust
THIS FORM FURNISHED BY TICOR TITLE INSURERS

For Value Received, the undersigned hereby grants, assigns and transfers to   Southwest Funding

all beneficial interest under that certain Deed of Trust dated   December 21, 1989
executed by   DAVID J.   AND DENISE R.
      Joint Tenants   , Trustor ,
to   SOUTH COAST TITLE COMPANY   , Trustee,
and recorded as Instrument No. 90000513 on Jan. 2, 1990   in Book/Reel _____ ,
Page/Image _____ , of Official Records in the County Recorder's office of   ORANGE
County, California, describing land therein as:

      More particularly described in said deed of trust.
      Commonly known as 827 N. Adlena Dr.   , CA
Together with the note or notes therein described or referred to, the money due and to become thereon with interest, and all rights accrued or to accrue under said Deed of Trust.

Dated   December 10, 1991

Long Kim   Tuong Nan Thi

FOR CORPORATE ACKNOWLEDGEMENT

Through the Courtesy of
SOUTH COAST
TITLE COMPANY

STATE OF CALIFORNIA   )
County of   Orange   )
)
On   December 11, 1991   before me, the undersigned, a Notary Public in and for said State,
personally appeared   LONG KIM
personally known to me or proved to me on the basis of satisfactory evidence to be the person(s) whose name(s) is/are
subscribed to the within instrument and acknowledged to me that he/she/they executed the same in his/her/their authorized capacity(ies), and that by his/her/their signature(s) on the instrument the person(s), or the entity upon behalf of
which the person(s) acted, executed the instrument.

personally
he within
he person
  executed
to its by-

─── Notary Seal ───

WITNESS my hand and official seal.
Signature Elizabeth L. Williams

OFFICIAL SEAL
ELIZABETH L. WILLIAMS
NOTARY PUBLIC - STATE OF CALIFORNIA
PRINCIPAL OFFICE IN
ORANGE COUNTY
My Comm. Expires April 30, 1994

personally
the basis
nowledged

Notary Public in and for said County and State

Long Kim
FOR PARTNERSHIP ACKNOWLEDGEMENT

STATE OF CALIFORNIA
COUNTY OF _____ } SS.
On _____ before me,
the undersigned, a Notary Public in and for said State, personally
appeared _____

personally known to me or proved to me on the basis of satisfactory evidence to be the person___ who executed the within
instrument as _____ of the partners of the partnership that executed the within instrument, and acknowledged to
me that such partnership executed the same.
WITNESS my hand and official seal.

Signature _____

(This area for official notarial seal)

Title Order No. _____   Escrow or Loan No. _____

THE OFFSET STATEMENT

Before a note purchase, the note buyer will want to be sure what the note seller has told him or her is consistent and truthful. The note buyer should therefore have the note seller fill out an offset statement.

This is a very important form and there are several crucial points to include in an agreement to purchase a note. The note buyer will want to be sure that the note seller and the payor agree about what the latest status of the note is. This includes the interest, how much the payments are, when the next payment is due, when the note matures, the balance due, and other important note features.

The note buyer can have the parties sign it or have their representative (title officer or real estate attorney) contact the person who owes the money on the note and have them fill out and sign an offset statement. The note buyer will want one of these statements signed by the property owner who owes the money and another by the person who is selling the note. This way there won't be any disputes later about the principal balance, number of remaining payments, or any special clauses.

What if the property owner (payor) does not agree with the offset statement and does not agree to sign it? What can the note buyer do? They can buy that note based on what the note seller represented. Then, if the payor does not pay for any reason – for example, the payor disputes the amount they owe – the note buyer would have to work that out with the note seller. In the meantime, the note seller would have to keep the buyer's note current, or the buyer could foreclose.

NOTICE OF TRANSFER OF LOAN AND NEW PAYEE LETTER

When I buy notes this is one my favorite letters to send. It's called the Notice of Transfer of Loan And New Payee. This lets the payor know that from now on they will send the payments to the note buyer and where to send those payments to. The buyer will send this letter (or have their escrow agent send it) to the payor once the transaction has been completed. Additionally, with this letter, the note buyer may also write a letter saying, "Would you like to pay off this note early?" The note buyer buys the note at a discount and then the payor refinances and pays off the note in full soon after – that's a home run and a really quick cash profit.

BECOMING THE PAYOR

In the previous deal, I was the note buyer. Remember, back when I started there was no network of buyers, so in order to make money you needed to take on the risk and buy them yourself. Thank goodness that has all changed since 1995 and the launch of my nation wide buying service.

Now, in this example, I want to share with you a deal where I became the payor. That's right, I used seller financing to help me purchase a property and gave the seller a better deal than he could hope for. It was a win-win situation all around.

Now, this deal is a big one – $4 million in fact – but that doesn't mean the principles of this can't be applied to almost any real estate deal… modest or enormous. The property that I purchased is a 46,000 square-foot office building that is now the home office of Dalbey Education. It's a fascinating building that used to be an aircraft parts assembly facility. Even now, it has giant cranes hanging from the ceiling that add a unique ambiance to the office.

The building had a listing price of $3.75 million, but I offered $4 million. It sounds crazy, but this is where creative deal structuring and seller financing turn this deal into a work of art.

When I got in touch with the seller, I discovered he wanted to use the proceeds from the sale to invest and that he was hoping for an 8% return on it. So, I made him an offer he couldn't refuse – an offer of $250,000 over his asking price if he would accept no money down and if he financed the sale himself at a 9% interest rate. I offered him MORE money than he wanted at a BETTER interest rate.

Of course the seller was interested when he heard this. What a great deal for the him, right? And think about the profit potential for you as a finder if you found this note. But this also turned out to be a terrific arrangement for me as well. There were advantages for me over a traditional bank-financed purchase.

A bank may have required a 25% down payment on a commercial property like this. So, through a traditional bank loan, I would need to come up with $937,500 (25% of $3.75 million) up front. Using a seller financed IOU, I was able to purchase a more expensive property and potentially more profitable property. I got more bang for my buck!

Not only is the office building in a prime location, I also knew that the area surrounding the property had some major development planned. A retail complex, restaurants, banks, hotels, and an events complex would soon be built in the area, undoubtedly causing the property to appreciate rapidly.

The deal worked out great for both the seller and me. The seller accepted $4 million for the property ($250,000 more than his asking price), no money down and carried the financing (9% interest over ten years). Twelve months after I purchased the property, the retail park and events center were completed, causing the building to appreciate dramatically; it actually appraised for double the purchase price.

I then went to the bank and refinanced the building which appraised for $7.2 million and I was able to pull out $2.6 million in cash, 100% tax free.

This "$4 million deal" is the perfect example of "working smarter, not harder" to get ahead. I'm not talking about making a few extra dollars when selling a home, but leveraging the concept of creative seller financing to put everyday people in charge of capital and resources that could potentially be worth tens of thousands of dollars!

This type of situation can happen every day, which means notes are created all the time. You never know, a multi-million dollar deal like this one could just be waiting to be found. Any note you find can be profitable for you... so it's time to discover just how you can become a note finder.

Exploring Your Role As A Note Finder

The concept of making big cash profits by finding notes and referring them to buyers, is the heart of *The Real Estate Secret*. This simple finder arrangement is the easiest and most practical approach for making a profit on any deal. Find a note, refer the note to buyers, and make a quick cash profit! Now, as I mentioned, we have several ways to profit in the seller financed real estate note business, but the Find Them, List Them, and Make Money method is the best way to get started with no money of your own!

The primary attractions of *The Real Estate Secret* is the "ease of entry" and the fact that none of the finding activities involve acting on the behalf of others. We are simply independent note finders, who make a profit for bringing basic information and knowledge to note buyers. It is this information and knowledge that allows us to make deals happen.

In this chapter, you will find all of the documents you need to help you earn quick cash profits. Please read through this chapter thoroughly because it is important to understand what's involved to be successful in this business.

KISS - KEEP IT SIMPLE SAM!

The Real Estate Secret offers a prospecting system that will eliminate both the need and the inclination for the time-consuming and psychologically stressful ramifications of the traditional "salesmanship" methods. We use this system to quickly screen for high probability prospects – a system that focuses our time on quickly determining whether the note is viable, and whether we can satisfy that note seller's needs.

If you look through the five types of note holders I talk about on page 74-75, you can easily see that this system makes it impossible to face rejection. If the note holder doesn't have a need, or you can't help them with the need they have, you should move on.

I can tell you this – McDonald's doesn't sell many hamburgers to people who aren't hungry, despite the millions of dollars they spend on advertising. And they aren't selling many hamburgers to people who are looking for a steak and lobster dinner.

But the last time I looked, they are still selling a boatload of hamburgers. They must be doing something right.

Just like McDonald's, start with the people who are interested and need your services and grow from there. Take a minute to learn the easy things and then you'll have the knowledge to understand the more complicated stuff.

So, don't leave town without your suitcase – get as ready as possible. You'll want to go through the rest of this book, and grab hold of these concepts that could open the door to your financial independence, and a whole lot of fun too.

A REAL ESTATE SECRET SUCCESS STORY

"This information gave me everything I needed to know! I've made $13,819.02 so far."

- Student, Susie S., Arkansas

THE GROUND FLOOR

When you are first starting out in the note business, you cannot possibly know or understand how to work with every type of real estate note out there. It may very well be that you don't even want to. But, you can get off the ground and start applying the information in *The Real Estate Secret.* That's right, by learning the most basic methods and techniques for moving forward on just one or two types, you can get started. This will put you in a position to earn while you learn, and then grow your business according to how you see fit.

This will also help keep you from trying to do too much at once, causing you to become overwhelmed and frustrated. Remember, Rome wasn't built in a day. And neither was any successful small business. Bill Marriott started with a simple little root beer stand long before launching the Marriott hotel chain. Dave Thomas, of Wendy's restaurant fame, started his career by opening The Ranch, a sit-down family diner.

Seeing how strong business was at a hot dog cart at the corner of Florence and Central in Los Angeles (one of his bakery route stops), Carl Karcher, the founder of Carl's Jr., and his wife, Margaret, made a leap of faith – they borrowed $311 on their Plymouth automobile, added $15 savings, and purchased the business. From the cart, they sold hot dogs, chili-dogs and tamales for 10 cents, and soda for a nickel. On his first day in the fast-food business, back in 1941, Carl Karcher took in $14.75. Within a few years, Carl and Margaret owned and operated four hot dog stands in Los Angeles. In 1945, the Karchers moved the short distance to Anaheim and opened their first full-service restaurant, Carl's Drive-In Barbeque. A year later hamburgers were added to the menu for the first time. What began as one man's entrepreneurial venture in 1941 has evolved into one of the most powerful businesses in the quick-service restaurant industry.

He certainly didn't start out that way. He started with the idea of building a successful business and he didn't try to do it over night. He started small and over time his business grew. In fact, it took 15 years for Carl to open his second restaurant.

Most businesses grow this way. They start small and overcome any obstacles on their way to success. The key is that the business owners don't give up. They set their eyes on the prize and stay focused until they achieve their goals.

Unfortunately, some people starting out in the note business try do everything at once and attempt to achieve their long term goals overnight. And when they don't see money falling from the sky right away, they give up. Don't let this happen to you. This is the GREATEST business in the world and it can provide you income month after month if you just stick with it. It's simple, fun, and something you can teach others to do in your family. The note business has been around since the beginning of time and will continue to be around long after we're gone.

Your goal when starting out, is to make money and your long term goal is to make a fortune. So get started and stay focused on your goals. Remember, all you have to do is find notes... find out as much as you can about those notes and refer them to buyers and wait for the check to come in.

FIND THEM! LIST THEM! MAKE MONEY!
Laying The Foundation

What I want to do first is make sure you have a very firm grasp on the simplest part of the note business. The reason I want to keep you focused on simplicity is because over the years, I have discovered that the one thing that holds people back in life is FEAR. I won't even bother going into all the possible "what-if's" that cause fear... because it doesn't matter.

The information I am going to share with you now will help you to overcome any fear you might have. Having this understanding will allow you to easily overcome what I believe are the two most common obstacles that hold people back from getting out there and grabbing their piece of this incredible opportunity:

1. Lack of knowledge

2. Fear of rejection

By carefully studying the basic information in this chapter, you will quickly come to recognize that when you finish this book, you will have more than enough knowledge to get started in building your financial future – a future you can be proud of and count on for years to come.

You will also see that it is impossible to face any kind of rejection! Yes... that's what I said. No rejection, zero, nada... because, when you follow the few simple secrets I am about to share right here, you will see that rejection cannot exist using this approach. It simply is not an option. And if rejection is not an option, it is impossible to fear it, right? Does that make sense to you?

Your first reaction might be disbelief. Okay… I'll grant you that for the next few minutes, because you aren't yet familiar with the things I am going to share with you.

So… let's start at the beginning. At the most basic level, particularly as a beginner note finder, your most important function is also the easiest. All you really need to learn to do is conduct investigations – i.e. gather meaningful information. This information is our stock-in-trade. We develop it, we package it, and we present it to note buyers.

This is our primary role in the seller financed real estate note industry: the value we bring to the table that allows us to make a "profit." No matter how much we want to grow, no matter how much experience we eventually gain, the process is ALWAYS the same for every real estate note, no matter what kind. We need to gather meaningful, relevant information as efficiently as possible.

First, you need to find out as much about the note as possible. As you can see from the list below, there is nothing too complicated about this, right? Nothing more than a little common sense. You are just asking the seller what is for sale. Here are a few of the simple questions will allow you to fill out the necessary information on the NOTE ANALYSIS WORKSHEET (the process of filling out the Note Analysis Worksheet which we'll cover later in the book) and can ultimately lead to your profits.

- What is the interest rate on the note?
- What is the payment amount on the note?
- How long is the term (original length) of the note?
- What is the original amount of the note?
- Is this the 1st or 2nd loan?
- What was the down payment amount?
- What was the sale price of the property?
- What type of property is it?
- What is the property address?

- What was the date of sale?

- What was the date of the first payment?

- Are the payments on time?

- What day of the month are the payments due?

Once you have collected this important information, you will simply list what you gathered on a nationwide buyer's network where buyers are waiting to bid and purchase the note you just found. It's that simple.

It's kind of like buying a car and before you would make an offer for that car you would ask the seller a few questions, right? Such as...

- What's the year? Year – early 90's (answer not specific enough)
- What's the make? Make – I think it's a Nissan, or a Honda (Which is it?).
- What's the model? Model – hmmm, a Cavalier (but Nissan doesn't make that model, and neither does Honda).
- What's the mileage? Mileage – oh, somewhere around 75,000, 95,000... somewhere in there.
- What type of interior? Interior – leather I think, it's definitely not cloth (What about vinyl?).

Pull out the old Kelley Blue Book (a price guide for cars) and try to find out what the car is worth with that information. It's impossible to do, right? Mr. Seller has to tell us what he really has for sale before we can start figuring out what a buyer may want to pay for it.

Now... think this part through. You are trying to find a note to list for a buyer. You can see that the information we are gathering about the note is what most note buyers will need to make a decision as to whether or not they will buy the note.

You don't have to sell the buyer anything. The information you provide either sells the note, or it doesn't. All you have to do is gather, package, and submit the information accurately and thoroughly. We can see that from this perspective, we don't need to have a great deal of knowledge to get started. Since we are not selling anything, we cannot face rejection. Since we cannot face rejection, we cannot be afraid of being rejected. How can we be afraid of something that cannot happen?

Now, to make sure you understand and believe this, let's take this process of simplicity one step further!

High Odds Note Finding

While you are finding out all about the note, one of your most powerful strategies for achieving success, in referring it to a buyer, is to find out about the note seller's motivation level.

Why is he/she interested in hearing an offer? How much cash does he/she need? What are his/her expectations?

Why do we want to know about their expectations? Because we know that almost any note holder would like to get a free "quote" for their note. That's human nature. But shopping quotes is not the same as selling notes – and nobody pays you for chasing your tail! It stands to reason that we can't do much note referring until we have some note holders to work with.

While most note holders are potential note selling prospects, not all are high-odds prospects.

Most note holders are going to fall into one of five categories, ranked here by priority:

1. Some prospects already need and want the service we offer. That group is ready to sell. These are the high probability prospects and we should devote our time, effort, and resources to them.

2. Some prospects need and want the service we offer, but won't sell. In other words, these prospects prefer another note finder. This group has potential, but only if we can change their mind and turn them into high-probability prospects BEFORE they decide to actually work with the other note finder.

3. Some prospects need what we offer, but do not want to sell their notes – at least, not now. This group is similar to group #2 above.

4. Some prospects do not need to sell their notes, and they do not want to sell them – at least not now. They don't mind holding the note and/or they like having the monthly income. They are not prospects right now, and might never be. Only time will tell. We need to spend less time on this group than we spend on groups #1, #2, and #3.

5. Some prospects need and want what we offer, but don't feel they can afford to accept the market value of their note. Most of the time these are low-probability prospects because we can't help them right now, but we can potentially help them in future.

The main reason why note holders sell their notes is because they need cash now. This need could be related to a problem they have to solve, or an important objective related to something else in their life. Other sellers are "don't wanters" – i.e., someone who never wanted the note in the first place. We want to focus our efforts on note holder prospects that need, want, and can afford to accept our note offers.

The closer a prospect fits that description, the higher the odds they will sell their note. That makes a note holder a high-odds prospect. Just because a note holder is willing to give you the opportunity to look for a bid on the note, does not turn a jar of fish eggs into a tin of caviar. But all notes can be sold *IF* they are viable, *IF* the note holder is motivated to sell the note, and *IF* the note holder can afford to accept your offer.

Now you can see that high odds note finding is not merely finding note holders, but also finding prospects likely to sell. Our objective then is to quickly reach an agreement with the note seller and move on to another deal.

Now, you might have figured that even the most serious note seller will sometimes get mixed up. They forget what is important, don't know what is important, or are afraid of the process. After all, not many note sellers know about the note buying process. But they are still note sellers, right?

And not many of them have made a career of selling notes… so, it stands to reason that they don't know much about the selling process.

So, you are going to run into folks who don't know as much as you know. Many sellers don't know much about the selling process and they don't know what to expect. First question they ask is "How much will you offer me for my note?" They just don't know any better, or they would tell you about their note first. The only answer you really can give them is "Without knowing what you have there is no way to know."

Think about it this way:

- How much for a piece of real estate? (House? Office building? Shopping center?)

- How much for a pair of shoes? (What kind of shoes? Keds? Timberlands?)

- What does a computer cost? (Notebook or desktop? PC or Mac?)

- What does a car cost? (What kind of car? Mileage? New or used?)

- How much for a set of golf clubs? (Kmart or Calloway?)

Does that make sense to you?

Q: What is the average amount of money note sellers receive for their note?

A: There is no average amount because the prices can vary widely. With real estate notes there are residential notes, commercial notes, land notes, and special-use property notes. What kind of note is it? Great, tell me more...

Here are some special characteristics the pricing depends on:

- The interest rate, other terms, and conditions of the property itself

- Who is living in the property (Is the property owner occupied or non-owner occupied?)

- The payment history on the note

- The current value of the property

- The number of monthly payments that have been made

- The payor's credit

- The payor's down payment

- The payor's income history

- The lien position of the note (Is it a first position or a second position note?)

- If it is a second position note what are the interest rate, term, loan amount, payment amount, and payment history of the first position loan

The questions above and a note information list I provided earlier in this book will be the backbone for any interview you conduct with a seller.

From this point on, it is a very simple process to fill in a few minor gaps, or adjust to different sellers' personalities.

What if the note holder wants to know all about you? That's okay to a point... but remember, if the note holder wants the best offer and you can get them the best offer, you really do not need to spend too much time making friends. So, tell them what you do. There is nothing wrong with that. However, there is no need for a drawn out question and answer session about you.

Here's an example of how to effectively answer a note seller's question about you:

Note Seller: Are you a broker or a buyer?

You: Actually, I am neither. I help note holders sell their future payments by referring them to buyers interested in payments secured by real estate. Have you ever considered selling your note before?

Also, because all transactions are put into escrow – just like in any real estate transaction – you are 100% protected and get what we agree upon.

As a matter of fact, in order to be of any benefit to you, I have to ASK you a few questions so I know exactly what's for sale. Why are you interested in receiving an offer? How much cash do you (they) need? How soon do you need the money?

From this information, I'll better understand the situation and in the long run do my best to meet your expectations. Nothing else really matters, right?

Note Seller: I have a $2 million real estate note here... I'm not going to turn that information loose with just anybody!

You: I completely understand your concerns. After all, I value the privacy of my personal business too. I don't need – or want – any sensitive information though. Names, phone numbers, and street addresses are not necessary for me to evaluate your note and give you a preliminary offer. I simply need to know about the note itself, the payor, and the property, okay?

Go back through the checklist and you'll notice that nothing there is too private? If the seller were selling you a car, you need to know the year, make and model, right? How much mileage too, right?

Keeping that in mind, you need to continuously focus on one thing: ASKING QUESTIONS. You want the note holder talking about 75% of the time... and you want their discussion focused on one thing – ANSWERING YOUR QUESTIONS about the note... and about his or her motivations for selling the note. If they are serious about selling the note, they will appreciate and respect your business-like approach. If they are not serious, it will not matter what approach you use. So keep it simple and to the point.

Is this note deal an excellent prospect? Maybe... maybe not. You won't know until you find out the answers to the questions you'll need to ask.

A truly serious note seller only cares about three things:

1. How much will you pay for my note?
2. How fast can I get my money?
3. How will I get what you're promising me?

To answer any questions, you simply go right back to square one. You need to know EXACTLY what the seller has for sale.

If your seller is hesitant in providing answers, or is not cooperating in moving forward and putting a note sale together, the safest assumption is that the seller is not really ready to sell the note. You can give them the benefit of the doubt at outset, and maybe spend a second interview with them. But, if you have spent longer than 15 minutes doing anything other than gathering answers to the questions you have… you aren't talking to a "note seller" – you're talking to someone who is wasting your time. Let it go and move on to the next potential deal and you can follow up with them in a month or two.

TEN SIMPLE STEPS TO MAKING QUICK CASH PROFITS

1. Find a note:

    a.   Search your county courthouse or use *Finding IOUs Easy* (**www.iou-finder.com**) to locate note holders in your area

    b.   Look in the newspaper for sellers – large and small papers both work

    c.   Contact attorneys, CPAs, mortgage brokers, realtors, and other professionals to solicit referrals – you can accomplish this by sending a postcard or calling

    d.   Use any of the 30 ideas I give you in Chapter 6 – How to Make Money Working with Seller Financed IOUs

2. Determine the value of the real estate note:

    a.   Fill out the NOTE ANALYSIS WORKSHEET (Covered in Chapter 7 – The Note Finder's Resource Kit)

    b.   Submit the note to buyers at **www.notenetwork.com/Noteservice**

    c.   See what offers you receive – depending on the type of note, it may take 24-72 hours

    d.   Consider all the prices offered by potential buyers

    e.   Choose the best offer

    f.   Deduct your finder's fee from the buyers's offer , this reduced figure will be your offer to the note seller (I recommend a minimum of $2000 to $5000 per deal)

3. Call note seller back to make the offer on their note:

    a.   If the note seller agrees to sell – proceed to Step 4

    b.   If the note seller declines to sell – follow up with note seller in 30 days to see if they changed their mind

4. Send initial paperwork to the note seller:

    a.   COMMITMENT LETTER filled out with the note seller's and your information (Page 148-150)

    b.   COVER LETTER TO THE COMMITMENT LETTER (Page 151)

    c.   INFORMATION REQUEST FORM (Page 152)

5. Get signed paperwork back from note seller along with necessary documentation:

    d.   Make sure the paperwork is filled out correctly and you have received everything requested

6. Send initial paperwork to the note buyer (wait to move forward until you receive signed documents back):

    a.   NON-CIRCUMVENT AGREEMENT filled out with appropriate information (Page 153-155)

    b.   PAYOUT AGREEMENT filled out with the buyer's information and your information (Page 156)

7. Forward all documents from the INFORMATION REQUEST FORM to the note buyer:

    a.   Make sure to keep a copy of all paperwork for your own records

8. Note buyer will open escrow to purchase:

    a.   Buyer handles all the paperwork – you do nothing at this point

9. Transaction takes place:

    a.   Buyer gets the real estate note and future payments

    b.   Seller receives their check for the sale

    c.   You receive a check valued at the dollar amount agreed on

10. Cash your check and find more deals!

And the real beauty here is if you ever have a question simply pick up the phone and give us a call or send us an email and we'll be happy to help you.

A REAL ESTATE SECRET SUCCESS STORY

"There is virtually no risk because I don't have any money invested out of my pocket at all. I've made over $46,006.25 in profits so far."

- Student, Darrell S., Washington

CHAPTER 4

Insider Secrets

A REAL ESTATE SECRET SUCCESS STORY

"This information included in the book has really changed our lives. We're having a good time doing this business and don't ever see us quitting. We've made over $227,921.00 and it works just like Russ said it would."

-Students, Mike & Betty C., Iowa

PROVEN MONEY MAKING TECHNIQUES FROM MY TOP STUDENTS!

I am sure you have noticed that throughout this book there are quotes from some of my most successful students. These students started the same way you are now, by reading the information contained in this book. Then they went out and put it all into action and made money.

To help you achieve the same level of success as my top students, I have included transcripts from interviews my team and I conducted with them. I want you to focus on what worked for them and the tips and tricks they used to get their businesses off the ground. Remember, it's better to work smart and learn from their successes as you work towards your own goals.

MIKE AND BETTY C., Iowa

Mike and Betty have profited over $227,921.00 since starting in the note business and have closed 49 note deals.

Interviewer: You know we've watched you from the very start. I think your smallest deal that you ever submitted to me was $475.00 dollars but then you look down the line here, the deal last week or so was $21,600.00 dollars plus!

Betty: Right.

Interviewer: My goodness, what kind of deal was that?

Mike: It was a 60 unit, brick apartment building.

Interviewer: You're of course in our Million Dollar Club and you've really kind of climbed the ranks slow pace. It was not an over night thing that happened for you guys.

Betty: No, but this last year has totally been different.

Interviewer: It really has been, let's just looking at your numbers here: $7,000.00, $7,000.00, $6,000.00, $7,000.00, $9,000.00, $4,000.00, $5,000.00, $21,000.00, it really has built up hasn't it?

Betty: Yes.

Interviewer: Have you changed your approach in terms of the marketing tools that you use? What marketing tools do you guys use?

Betty: Mostly professionals, attorneys…(Referral marketing)

Interviewer: What have you all done in terms of tangible courses?

Betty: We had counseling when we first started.

Interviewer: Are we talking about the coaching program?

Betty: Yeah.

Interviewer: Okay.

Betty: That was really helpful we had two coaches and both of them were really good.

Interviewer: And is this the only course that you actually have taken besides reading the book?

Betty: Yeah.

Interviewer: What would you say about the coaching program to somebody just thinking about getting into it. What are the benefits of being in the course?

Betty: We really gained a lot from having a coach. You see we had a strong background in real estate but soon came to realize that the note business is in a field of it's own. Being a part of the coaching program allowed us to ask questions along the way – and knowing that we had someone there to guide us through any pitfalls we might come across was reassuring.

Interviewer: Do you think it's important to have someone to kind of walk them through the steps?

Betty: Definitely.

Interviewer: You've been to multiple Workshops, you've heard Russ' presentation about the importance of goal setting. Do you guys still reevaluate your goals and reset goals along the way?

Betty: Well we do because we usually meet them far quicker then we ever think we're going to, we really do! We want to be able to be totally out of debt, have our home paid for and just be more financially independent. That's kind of a broad goal, I know but, we've set goals as we went a long with this and with our business.

Interviewer: Yeah, Betty you were just mentioning that you have accomplished your goals way ahead of your estimated time line, has that come as a surprise to you in this business?

Betty: Yes and no. I mean I knew that it should work and if we were patient, the business would start building up, just like any other business. It's just better than I thought it was going to be.

Interviewer: Is this something you're going to do for the future now? Is this your future?

Betty: It will be because managing apartments, it requires physical work, and being away more and thinking about it as we get older, having this to do because there's no physical work to it, I don't think there's going to be any age limit to it and we're the type of people that keep wanting to have challenges, we really like this, so I can't see us ever quitting this.

Interviewer: For somebody out there that's reading this, what can you share with them, what do they have to do to be successful in this business?

Betty: They have to be willing to learn, take constructive criticism, listen to ideas, and talk to people who are in the business and who have made it work. Use those ideas, be open to try them, be willing to learn is the biggest thing!

CHUCK L., California

Chuck L. spent over 17 years as a civil engineer, until recently. Chuck said "enough was enough" as he was tired of working long hours and making somebody else rich. So he put his long time dream of working for himself into motion. Profiting $64,847.92 in 11 note deals, Chuck said "it was the freedom to care for his family, the freedom to travel, and the freedom to work from home!" that gave him the inspiration to make the note business his full time profession.

Interviewer: I know that when we last spoke, you were in Alaska.

Chuck: That's right, yeah. I was able to spend 3 months up there this summer. And, actually close a couple of deals.

I closed those deals in a very remote cabin in Alaska. I actually, I went, its a family owned cabin and I had to set up a satellite Internet service.

But just by having the interent connection... And I did have a fax machine up there and we did have an old analog phone system. So I was able to fax and check email and just basically conduct business at our family's cabin. And it was, it was amazing. It is the freedom I was looking for. This business has afforded me the freedom to just do whatever I want anywhere in the world with just an Internet connection and a fax machine, I can just keep making money.

Interviewer: Yeah those two deals you closed while you were up camping out in Alaska – made you $14,669.00 dollars and some change.

Chuck: Yeah! It's pretty amazing!

Interviewer: How long have you been in the business?

Chuck: Since the end of the year in 2005 is when I first signed up as a student and then I did participate in the coaching program.

Interviewer: How long were you an engineer, Chuck?

Chuck: Um, 17 years.

Interviewer: You had to really dig deep to, to resign, because that was your profession.

Chuck: Uh, Yeah. It was hard, you know? And I was very comfortable; I was very good at what I did. It was a safe government job I guess, very secure. But, I was not happy with it because I didn't have any freedom and I didn't have time to spend with my family or travel as much as I wanted to. All of that security, might be nice if you, if you need that security, but I was looking for more freedom and quite frankly an opportunity to make even more money without as much effort. The note business that I've started allows me to do that. I have the potential to far exceed my engineering income and if I want to work that hard to do it. And at the same time, I have the power to choose if I want to work less and not make as much money, that I can do that as well. And still travel and do things I want to do.

Interviewer: So you do the business full-time now?

Chuck: I wouldn't say full time. But it's my only job I guess, if you want to think of it that way. It's more like a part time job, you know, I think I can probably have well in excess of a six figure income with it, if I was working 40 hours a week at it.

Interviewer: So what marketing tools do you currently use with your business?

Chuck: I like to write letters to people that are carrying notes, and I get their information from the courthouse website. Basically all you need is a name and an address. I've found that hand written letters work the best. I get better responses from hand written letters versus like, mass mailings or mass mailing postcards.

Interviewer: Do you think that's because they are more personable?

Chuck: Yeah, I think people... and they are more professional, I write a very professional letter, and I let people know that I'm not a large institution that is sending them junk mail. I make myself really approachable in the letters so they know they can call me and talk to me directly, versus going through some phone bank system. Now I am also relying on referrals in my own community. I visit attorney's offices and accountants. I think accountants are the best because almost everybody has an accountant. Especially if they have income property or they own real estate that they have sold. The accountants tend to get all the questions. Not every body has a lawyer, but almost everyone has an accountant. So when the person who carried back the mortgage has a financial or legal question, sometimes they ask their accountant.

Interviewer: How much budget do you allocate a month for your business in terms of marketing?

Chuck: A few hundred dollars a month. If I had to average it out over the year maybe, four or five hundred a month, in mailing and you know FedEx, letters and postage. I do a few post cards every once and a while, though the letter I think stands out more. I do get a higher response rate with letters. I would say between eight percent and ten percent, if I mail 200 letters, I will get anywhere between 15-20 calls.

Interviewer: How many hours a week did you put in as an engineer?

Chuck: Oh, 40-50 on average.

Interviewer: And now in the note business?

Chuck: Oh, less than half of that. If I work 5 hours a day, that's a big day, and that's a 20 hour work week. Yesterday for example, I think I worked maybe a couple of hours and then I worked on the roof. If I was working as an engineer I would have had to take a vacation day or get approval to go home and take care of my house. It's just silly, I felt like I was in prison. Like, I had to get permission to do everything. I felt like I was doing time there eight or nine hours a day. I looked at all the people who worked thirty or forty year careers in that organization and then they retired, and I looked at the lifestyle they were living and their financial situation and I knew I didn't want that. And now that I've learned what this business is all about I know that I can create a better future for my family and myself, I have no doubt in my mind whatsoever.

Interviewer: Speaking about futures, have you set goals for your business?

Chuck: I have. My long term goal within the next year to two years, I want to gross over $200,000 dollars a year in income because there is such a huge volume of notes out there.

CHARLIE T., New York

Charlie T. is an 84 year old immigrant from Puerto Rico, a former World War II B17 crew member and a survivor who spent 86 days in a POW camp. After all shouldn't he be thinking about spending his senior years resting and taking it easy? "No way!" say's Charlie, "I still have a lot of living to do." Charlie found a potential note deal while doing courthouse research. After contacting the holder of the note he found he was able to close the deal and make $1,343.34 in the process.

Interviewer: I know that you finally closed your first deal?

Charlie: Yep, I made $1,343.34 dollars out of it.

Interviewer: Was it a hard deal?

Charlie: It wasn't really hard, I learned a lot and I am a little more experienced now.

Interviewer: What type of deal was it, was it an SFR?

Charlie: Oh yeah, yeah. A single family residence.

Interviewer: How long did it take you to close that deal?

Charlie: Oh I would say about, uh, about three weeks.

Interviewer: How long have you been applying this information?

Charlie: I'm pretty new with this thing.

Interviewer: Well how long?

Charlie: A couple of months, two or three months, I guess.

Interviewer: Do you do this business on a full time or part time basis?

Charlie: Uh, part time.

Interviewer: What do you do full time?

Charlie: Nothing, I'm retired.

Interviewer: You sound too young for that Charlie

Charlie: I am 84 yrs old.

Interviewer: What did you do before you retired?

Charlie: I worked for the post office. I am from Puerto Rico, I was born in Puerto Rico, raised in New York City, and I came here when I was nine years old. Got drafted, I was in the air force; I am a Second World War vet. I got shot down in a B17 and I became a prisoner of war. I worked in a POW camp for 86 days and here I am, by god's grace, I am still here.

Interviewer: Why did you decide to get into the note business?

Charlie: Well they sent me that little booklet. I started to read about it and it got very interesting; I think it's a great deal.

Interviewer: How did you find that deal?

Charlie: I went to the courthouse, I looked at the local courthouse records, I get my notes from there.

Interviewer: You mentioned courthouse marketing of course that's one of your marketing tools that you use, do you use any other marketing tools?

Charlie: Not right now, but starting next week I am going to work on my marketing plan for referrals and I will get in touch with CPA's, Attorney's, Real Estate Agents and so forth.

Interviewer: After you closed that deal, did it excite you about the business?

Charlie: I was excited about the business right from the beginning, now of course, I think it depends on the individual to be successful. But yeah, I think it's great. In the future depending on how things work, I'm thinking of getting the newsletter. That newsletter is terrific.

Interviewer: When you completed the book, did you feel that you could be successful in this business and you could do it?

Charlie: Yeah, I still do.

Interviewer: What does it take in your opinion to be successful in this business?

Charlie: Well first of all you have to like it, you have to believe that you're going to be successful because all it takes is your own particular effort to do so. You cannot fail if you're interested enough and want to succeed in it, you can't fail. You just can't fail.

LINDA C., Texas

Linda C. from Texas has lived a life only a few can dream of. An Air Force Academy graduate, over 20 years in corporate America as a systems engineer specializing in IT. She now calls the note business "her future." As a single mom and only in the note business for a short time, she recently closed her first deal taking only a few weeks to profit $1,493.72. Linda says, "You need to make an investment in your future and take advantage of the educational courses offered by Russ."

Interviewer: And how long have you been in the business?

Linda: Since the beginning of January.

Interviewer: 2007?

Linda: Yeah

Interviewer: You have done some fantastic work.

Linda: I have probably got 15 notes in various stages of work right now. Just a lot of things going on and I love it, absolutely love it.

Interviewer: You said, you know, I have been pretty lucky so far, how much does luck play into this business?

Linda: Well, I gotta tell you, I have worked my butt off so a lot of it is me working hard and developing an excellent reputation. Buyers love me and they love my notes because I do my homework and do what you guys taught me to do. You collect the information and you present it well and you will get buyers that will want to make you offers. I do a good job of collecting the info, I collect more then what is needed, I get a description of the SFR I really try to understand the motivations and expectations of the sellers I find out what the payors do for a living, I collect and do my homework. So I have been able to develop a really good reputation with many buyers.

Interviewer: Okay, let's back track just a second here. You started off with the book is that correct?

Linda: Yeah I got something in the mail from you guys and read it and ordered the books.

Interviewer: Where did it go from there? Now, have you used any other programs that we offer at Dalbey?

Linda: Yes, I also enrolled into the 5 month Protege program. I did the Protege workshop in early May, I did the Executive Fast Track and Triple Crown in late January and in February.

Interviewer: When you got the book, why was it that you had to go to Protege? What was missing in the basic manual?

Linda: I just wanted to learn more, fast. I wanted it now, I wanted to learn the business now. I am very assertive being an air force academy graduate and veteran, you know. I am very direct and I wanted to know the business fast. I was willing to pay for it. I tell everyone that I talk to, those workshops that I attended plus the Protege 5-month program where outstanding and worth it. I needed more depth and I needed it fast.

Interviewer: Do you do this business on a full time or part time basis?

Linda: No, full time.

Interviewer: What marketing tools do you use?

Linda: Let me open up my handy dandy things, I am tracking them all. Um, lets see, alright, so I have got the newsletters; I try to put out at least 100 a month. I am putting those out to referral networks, people, you know, the professionals. I also use a company they are doing banners and I can tell you that I have gotten one note through that I do postcards, I do flyers, if I am going to a grocery store, I put a flyer with pull tabs on the front of my windshield I put them in grocery stores, I post them anywhere I can. I do some free classified ads through ad post and um, free ads, I ordered car magnets for my brother's truck.

Interviewer: With this huge arsenal of materials to promote your business, you had to have sat down and established a monthly budget.

Linda: I don't have a set amount. I haven't established that. To me it's what makes sense to me given my current scenario. I did the business plan and all that, but I don't have a set amount.

Interviewer: First deal's down $1,493.72 dollars, what kind of deal was that?

Linda: It was an SFR, this note seller though, in NC, has other properties that he is going to list with me too. He liked the way I did business, we closed quickly and he is giving me another note.

Interviewer: Yeah how long did it take to close that note?

Linda: About two weeks.

Interviewer: Was it easy?

Linda: Yeah, yeah it was easy.

Interviewer: What about your goals? I know you set them.

Linda: Yeah. My goal when I started this was to make $5,000 a month by the end of the first year. I am going to be exceeding that. That was my immediate goal. I wanted to be able to live off it so that meant 5,000 a month by December 07. Now I have upped that to 15,000 a month. That's my goals, so in another six months I want to be making about 15,000 a month and I think that's do able.

Interviewer: When you first got the book, did you feel that you could do this business?

Linda: I did.

Interviewer: While we're talking about that very first note, somebody listening to us today, maybe in your position, hasn't closed that first note deal as of yet, what do they need to do to be successful in this business?

Linda: They need to know what to gather, and be able to gather it quickly and present it well. I mean everything you say is true. You need to know what to gather so you have got to have your ducks in line with the worksheet, the note analysis worksheet.

Interviewer: Are you having fun?

Linda: Oh you bet. I love it, I love this. I just love what I do here, I love it!

SCOT A., California

Scot A. from California has closed 26 deals profiting $63,352.06 mostly using print marketing materials such as postcards.

Interviewer: How long have you actually been in the note business?

Scot: I got the information a couple of years ago but I actually didn't start until that June, so it's been about just shy of a year and a half.

Interviewer: Looking back on the year and a half, has it been a good journey or a hard one?

Scot: Both. I've learned a heck of a lot. I mean the learning curve has been great and I enjoy that aspect of it. It didn't take off as quickly as I wanted but it's starting to really roll now. Gosh, I've got seven offers. So hopefully all of those will go through.

Interviewer: I know you just sent me the latest 2 deals, do you have a total amount if you put the 26 deals together, how much you've profited?

Scot: Um, just over $60,000. Isn't a whole lot, but I did some really small deals. And you just can't take much of a commission there or it's just going to kill the deal.

Interviewer: So how much was deal #9 for? Do you remember?

Scot: Just over $6,000.

Interviewer: Okay, and what about deal 10?

Scot: 900 and some dollars.

Interviewer: Yeah but you gotta really be proud of that, whether they're big or they're small you're…

Scot: It's still a check, I'll take it!

Interviewer: Exactly right. Your business is moving right along.

Scot: Exactly.

Interviewer: What do you think the hardest thing is about working with seller financed notes?

Scot: Oh, it's probably just waiting on documents. Everyone's in a hurry, you know, until you ask them for documents and then it takes forever. You know, that's not too bad. If you've got a bunch of deals going you just keep following up on people and make sure things happen in a timely manner, at least to the best of your ability. But not everyone has the same motivation to get it done when you want to get it done.

Interviewer: How do you find your deals? What's the common denominator in your deals?

Scot: Originally the first few deals I actually purchased leads and did a mailing. So I never touched them. The leads I purchased went right to a postcard company and they sent it out and I got my first few deals that way. But since then I do a ton of research at the county recorder. And I've covered 4 counties around me now, and I've gone back 2 years into each county. So I've created a huge database of people that have notes, and I just mail them out a letter originally and then follow up with a postcard about every 8-10 weeks.

Interviewer: You ever have to call the company for any kind of help or anything like that any more?

Scot: Once in a while. I'll have a question. Most of it now I think I've got it pretty well under control. But uh, yeah, it's nice to know that they're there and they can answer a question whether it's simple or hard and they're always there so why not use it?

Interviewer: You know you were explaining to me that you live in some of the most beautiful country in the world, there in Northern California. How does it feel working in a position here where you can live where you want to and do the job that you want to and not have to worry about doing it on somebody else's time or place.

Scot: It's great. My passion is working with horses, so I've got my horses out front, I've got an office on my property, and you know once I contact everyone and there's a lull, I go out and work with my horses, I mean that's fantastic.

BARBARA G., Pennsylvania

Barbara G., a house wife of 28 years with no college degree, has become one of Russ Dalbey's most successful note finders. To date, she has closed over 180 deals that made here $869,457.72.

Interviewer: How long have you been in the note business?

Barbara: 7 years.

Interviewer: Before you got involved in this note business, did you know anything about this business?

Barbara: No, not at all, nothing! Never even heard of it! I was an empty nester, both of my daughters had graduated from college and were out and I was saying, "Now what am I going to do with myself?"

Interviewer: So there you are, you're searching for something to do primarily.

Barbara: Correct.

Interviewer: There's a lot of home based business's out there, why did you choose the note business?

Barbara: Well to be honest with you, I didn't know what I was going to pick, and I knew I didn't want to punch the time clock somewhere. And so I let some time pass and sort of felt, "What can I do from home?" And it was ironic because it was like here it is a Sunday afternoon, at 2:00 in the afternoon in the winter time and it was cold out.

Interviewer: And you live up in Pennsylvania, right?

Barbara: I do… I remember it was cold out and there was this infomercial and I started watching it and I thought, "Hmm, this kind of sounds interesting" and my husband was there and I said, "Listen, listen to this" you know. And I jotted down the number and I continued to listening to it and I thought "Hmm this might be something that I could do" you know, "I don't know much about it, but I think I'm going to give them a call" and that's exactly how that went down. I actually called the number and um, asked a lot of questions and they said, "Well let me send you some information through the mail" and that's what they did, and well I guess really the rest is history. But I mean I felt it was something I could learn to do.

Interviewer: There you are you're watching television along with your husband; his name's John, isn't it?

Barbara: That's correct.

Interviewer: Yeah so there you are you're watching television. Russ Dalbey's on television, he's doing his show, what was said in that program, what did Russ say that intrigued you so much?

Barbara: I think the thing about the commercial that enticed me was that I came from a banking background okay, so I always was fascinated with numbers and stuff like that you know I was always fascinated but never really go to fulfill that because I got married young and had children. But I thought, "You know here's something to do with numbers, and real estate, and you can make some money at this, and I can do it from home and they were willing to help you." And it was just sort of a mixture of a lot of things that made me want to make that phone call.

Interviewer: After you initially took the plunge and you read the information, how long did it actually take you to become involved in the business and work with real deals and real money?

Barbara: I would say within 6 months. Within 6 months of getting the program and finding the time to do the program, reading the program, understanding the program, making the phone calls, getting myself set up (because I did not get right into it immediately, it took me a couple of months) so from the time I got the program from the time I really started to dive into it was about a 5 or 6 month period, but once I did, boom!

Interviewer: Did the materials and information provide you with the solid foundation of education and knowledge that enabled you to do this business?

Barbara: Yes, it did.

Interviewer: I just want to know, did our information, did it actually give you a foundation to do this business?

Barbara: Yes it did, it gave me a foundation to do this business yes. I mean it gave me the start to do the business. There were all these things that you needed to learn and if I had any questions. And I can remember you know calling up and asking questions and you know sometimes, I couldn't pick it up right away I'd get frustrated with myself, and get upset with myself and I can remember them saying, "Now, Barbara take your time, don't get yourself all worked up over this we'll get you through this, you'll understand it" you know. And that's what they did they really took the time to teach me to understand it you know? And let me just say, not just understand it, but to really understand it. So that way I could pass that on when I was doing the business you know? And to be able to communicate that.

Interviewer: So what I'm reading between the lines here, the company did supply you with support in getting your business going?

Barbara: Yes, absolutely!

Interviewer: Have you ever tried any other home based business like this?

Barbara: No.

Interviewer: This is your very first?

Barbara: Yeah, my very first home based business since I was a teenager. I did start a business when I was a teenager actually. I was actually 18, 19 years old and I started a home based business then in a college town but this is altogether… after that no, this is it. This is it.

Interviewer: I always like to use you as an example because of the line you told me 7 years ago about being an empty nester because that makes a lot of sense and it applies to a lot of people out there doing this business. There are a lot of mothers out there where their children have left, they're looking for something to do. Give me an example on how the business has actually affected your life. Has this been a real positive experience?

Barbara: You know this has been the most positive experience, other then having children that I've ever had. I mean the respect that I've earned in this business from a lot of people is very important. This is a very small community okay, no matter where you are in the United States it doesn't matter it's still a small community to the point where people know each other. I've earned a lot of respect from a lot of people, I've met a lot of people in this business. I mean I get to meet a lot of people. Not just by phone, but actually physically meeting them. And I have got to do, and go places and see things that I've never would've dreamt I would've been able to do, never. All because of this business. But I have to say you know, I take pride in my business, and I work hard at this business, I love this business. I absolutely love it!

Interviewer: An opportunity to make this kind of money, has it made your life better?

Barbara: Oh absolutely.

Interviewer: Give me an example on how it's made your life better?

Barbara: Okay well let's see, we do a lot of trips. We have newer cars okay, my children are definitely benefiting. I have one daughter that lives in Florida for instance, so I can go down and see her at least 5-6 times a year, and just normal everyday things I don't have to worry about where the money's coming from for the refrigerator that might have broke, or the washer and dryer that might have gone bad, or you know anything! It's just there; it makes life so much easier!

Interviewer: You do a lot of traveling. Are you still able to do this business while out there on the road?

Barbara: Yes I am. People don't even know I'm traveling. The only way people know I'm traveling is they have to contact me by my cell phone. Because I have a computer laptop I take with me, so I email people, they don't know if I'm in Pennsylvania or if I'm in California. So nobody even knows there's a down time at all. I keep it up and I have no problem with doing that because it's easy, you know. When you have a laptop you can go anywhere and do this anywhere.

Interviewer: We are speaking about essential items for running a seller financed real estate note Business. If someone was listening to us today, they want to start the business, what pieces of equipment do they have to have to operate this business?

Barbara: Well they should have a computer. They have to have access to a fax, and they have to have a phone, long distance on their phone.

Interviewer: Are you a slave to this business or do you make your own shots in terms of how much you want to work?

Barbara: I make my own shots.

Interviewer: How much time do you spend dedicated to doing things business, say like on a daily basis?

Barbara: Well that's a tough question, it depends uh, yesterday I went bowling, went out to lunch and went shopping I didn't get back into my office until 2. Today I golfed until 12:30.

Interviewer: Life is rough there Barb!

Barbara: That's what my husband said, "Boy you had a tough day, golf today, bowling tomorrow." But some days I only work in a few hours, and other days I'll tell you honestly I can work 10 hours a day, it just depends. Because this business you never know how busy you're going to be each day, okay. But still, no matter how busy I am, I can still make my own hours.

Interviewer: There you go you mentioned another word that kind of sparked a kind of a nerve in my brain; you mentioned your husband.

Barbara: Yep.

Interviewer: I know he's involved in this business, how did he get involved in this business?

Barbara: You know how he got involved in this business? Is when he would come home from work, and I wasn't always right there to greet him at the door. He would say well I'm going to sit here and twiddle my thumbs while my wife's in there doing this business. So after about a year of that he said you know what, "Is there anyway you can teach me this business?" I said, "Yes, I think I can now, I think I feel comfortable enough that I could teach you this business." So it took me about 4 or 5 months because he did work full time and everyday he'd come home and I would teach him a little bit and a little bit more and a little bit more to the point now, when he comes home. He has a set schedule, he gets home about 3:30-4:00 and he goes right in, he has his own little space in the office now with the laptop that we use when we travel and he gets right on the business and he absolutely loves it.

Interviewer: I actually get a lot of comments about how nice your husband is.

Barbara: Oh really!?

Interviewer: Now you guys have obviously have split your business, I think he has the responsibilities of maybe contacting people at that point. Is that how that works? How do you split the business up between you and John?

Barbara: He has the responsibility of making a lot of the contacts, I'm in the back end of the business when it comes with John, because he doesn't have time to learn the back end of the business that would be the closing aspect of it. He's not here during the day so he'll make the initial contact the phone calls, the calculations on the note, getting the information, and stuff like that. I get the quotes. Then when deals get accepted then I take it from there, I do all the paperwork, all the closing aspects of it, and everything. Because like I said he doesn't have the time, he's gone during the day. So I do all of that. We call it "Him doing the front end and I do the back end."

Interviewer: What does John do for a real job?

Barbara: He is an electrician at a steel mill.

Interviewer: Now does he have enough time to do this business along with that business?

Barbara: Believe it or not, he does.

Interviewer: That's amazing.

Barbara: He makes time because he likes the business. I mean there are times he comes home and he's really, really tired and I'll say, "Why don't you take a break tonight?" He says, "No let me just rest my eyes for 20 minutes." And he'll shut his eyes for 20 minutes then off he goes and he'll get right into it. I mean sometimes I get upset with him because I'll say, "It's dinner are you going to come and eat?" And he likes getting on the phone talking to these people. I mean he likes doing that, I mean he just enjoys doing that.

Interviewer: When you guys stare at each other in the face and you have those dreamy eyes looking at each other, uh, do you ever think like, "John did you ever think we could make this kind of money doing this business?"

Barbara: No we never thought we could. I mean we never really had any idea of the potential this business had, I mean we really didn't. I don't think anybody does. I mean you can dream it or think it, but you know, it really does become a reality when you see it. It's really happening.

Interviewer: When you first read the information and you took a look at it; did you think you could be successful?

Barbara: Not at first, no. Not at first I didn't.

Interviewer: Well how did you convince yourself?

Barbara: Well actually what convinced me, I shouldn't say I convinced myself, after I started doing it and seeing how it worked, that's when I realized that I can do well in this business. That's when it hit me that, "You know what, I could really do this."

Interviewer: Can anybody do this business? Or does it take a person who has an advanced mathematical degree or a background in business management?

Barbara: You don't have to have a mathematical degree and I didn't or a business background, no. I was just a housewife, I never went to college so I was just a housewife for 28 years of my life so, I had no degree in anything, nothing. That's what flabbergasted me so much, that I could pick up on this.

Interviewer: As an empty nester, was there a necessity for you to have to make the money to help your families income and survive?

Barbara: No it wasn't a necessity, I mean I never worked during the raising of our children. It wasn't really a necessity it was like um, something that I needed to do for myself. I was young to the point that sitting at home wasn't the answer. Again I wanted to contribute so we could do extra things and have extra things and go extra places. You know, make life a little bit better then what we had, not that our life was bad, but I wanted to make it better.

Interviewer: Can you think of any business out there that would maybe take you less time and still allow you to make this kind of money?

Barbara: No, I can't think of any business, unless I hit the lottery for you know 100 million dollars but no, I can't think of any business.

Interviewer: Do you ever have people come up to you or communicate with you and maybe they're extremely skeptical about this business and they say to you, "Oh you're just a unique case, you know no one can really do this business." Have you ever had to defend this business and maybe help them over come that skepticism?

Barbara: Sure I have.

Interviewer: How do you do that?

Barbara: Well I tell people I say, "You know that there's a lot of potential in this business, okay? And if you work at it, you can make it whatever you want it to be, because it's your business." And I say you know here's how I explain it to people that I do business with. "You know we're all in this together, we're all in the same business okay and I'm here to help you, whether I do your deal or not, I'm here to help you get your deals done. With my experience and knowledge I'm happy to do that, okay?" And they'll say, "You're kidding" and I'll say, "No I'm not kidding you because people like that helped me. I know that you can become frustrated sometimes, okay? And it can seem like you know you don't know the answers to all these questions that you have going through your head and so that's why I try to tell people I can understand why you're skeptical, but let me make it easier for you." And that's what I do, I try to make it as easy as I can for people.

Interviewer: Do you consider yourself a part time person in this business?

Barbara: I consider myself, I don't work 40 hours a week, so I guess I consider myself part time. I'm here but I consider it part time.

Interviewer: We don't have enough time to talk about all the deals you ever did because that would fill up hours and hours of this conversation but let me kind of intrigue everyone here today and let's talk about how much money did you make on your largest deal?

Barbara: $25,000.00

Interviewer: Do you remember how long it took you to make that kind of money and what type of deal it was then?

Barbara: You know honestly and it's not that I'm bragging, I've done a lot of deals and of course you guys are aware of that. I do so many deals that I can't remember, I really can't remember. I wish I could um, and it's not a bad thing that I can't remember, I think it's a good thing that I can't remember because I do so many deals and I look at it a little bit differently now. I do deals, it doesn't matter what I make on them.

Interviewer: What type of deals do you like to do? You know you've got single family residence, you've got mobile homes, and you've got commercials. What is your favorite type of deal?

Barbara: I'm going to say single family right now. Single family's are my best money maker right now the SFR's.

Interviewer: What would you recommend for somebody just getting into this business in terms of ease and simplicity? What type of deal would that be?

Barbara: Single family. Single family residence is a lot easier to put together in my opinion then a commercial or a mobile home or land yes, single family.

Interviewer: What type of person couldn't succeed in this business?

Barbara: I don't know anybody that couldn't succeed in this business. Maybe a non-motivated person, I mean that doesn't want to do anything and then expects money to be dropped in their lap. I mean but if they're willing to put out some time and some energy and some effort anybody can do this business.

Interviewer: Somebody's out there listening to us Barb, thinking about becoming involved in the note business, what can you say to them about getting started? What do they have to do to be successful?

Barbara: Not to give up. Just have patience and not give up, because it can be done, I mean I would tell you there's probably a job out there that you can't get frustrated with but just not giving up. And keep going and keep going and keep going and you will prevail and that would be my biggest advice to anybody.

After all the comments you just read you should now understand in simple plan language exactly what you need to do to create the future you want.

Remember, everyone at Dalbey Education, the education and support network for Russ Dalbey's students, is here for your success. Please see page 196 to read about hundreds of additional money making success stories.

Getting Results and Making Money

I want to give you valuable tips and tools that will help you get your note finding business on the path to success. As the bottom line, keep in mind you don't have to learn everything to make money with notes. My bet is that very few of my students will ever learn all of this information – yet many will still make money. I just want to give you everything I've promised and more.

One favor I'd personally like to ask you – promise me and promise yourself that you will stay excited long enough to complete your first note deal. After that, you will be so excited and so happy that you will never want to do anything else.

MY HIDDEN MOTIVATION... REVEALED!

Everyone needs a mentor at some point. In fact, I firmly believe that getting help from the right source is absolutely key to achieving success! The truth is, I had a mentor who taught me everything I know about making money in the note business. It was my mentor's goal to guide me towards success, and my promise is to do the exact same for you. But you'll have to do your part. Money is not going to fall from the sky just because you read this information. You have to take some action, okay? And nothing makes me happier than hearing about another person who's been able to move closer to their dreams of financial independence through *The Real Estate Secret*!

Now I will give you a few tools you could use to start working with seller financed notes and potentially earn a lot of extra money – working in your spare time – starting today.

Please let us know if there's anything we can do to help you grow your business by sending us an email at **support@dalbeyeducation.com**. My staff and I truly care about your success, and we'll do everything we can to help you reach your financial dreams. We look forward to working with you and hearing about your success.

COURTHOUSE LEAD SHEET

This worksheet is intended to make your visit to the courthouse go smoothly while staying organized. Feel free to download as many copies of this worksheet as you need and carry it with you on every courthouse lead hunt.

Today's Date: _____

Document number: _____

The person receiving the payments – the mortgagee's information:
(This is the information you want, as this is the person you will mail or call.)

Name: _____

Address: _____

The person making the payments – the payor's information:
(In the event you'd like to refer to this information when talking to the note seller.)

Name: _____

Address: _____

Worksheets are available online at:

www.notefindersresourcekit.com

Just follow the simple directions on my website and we will email you copies of this and any other worksheet you may need.

THE TELEPHONE SCRIPT
Getting Information On A Note For Sale

Remember, you're getting paid for simply gathering information from someone who holds a note. It's very simple to do. The following script is what you will use to gather note information from the note holder. Once you get this information all you do is post it at **www.notenetwork.com/Noteservice** where buyers will bid on the note you found. Also, there is a worksheet that you will use called the NOTE ANALYSIS WORKSHEET where you will insert the answers to the questions below.

Introduction:

Hi **(Note Holder's First Name)**, this is **(Your Name)**. I'm interested in the property you sold recently. Are you still receiving monthly payments from that sale?

IF YES: I'd like to offer you a free quote to let you know what your payments are worth today (Proceed to question 1).

IF NO: What happened? Did they pay it off or was it refinanced?

*NOTE: When asking the following questions it is best to ask them in an informal manner. Also, be friendly while getting the information you need.

1. What kind of interest rate are you getting?_____

2. What is the payment amount?_____

3. How long is the term (original length) of the loan (note)? _____

4. What is the original amount of the loan (note)?_____

5. Is this the 1st or 2nd loan? _____

    5a. (If 2nd ask: What was the amount on the 1st position loan?)

    _____

6. What was the down payment the buyers paid? _____

7. What was the sale price of the property? _____

8. What is the property type (SFR, condo, commercial, or other)? ____

9. What is the property address? _____

10. Are the new buyers living there? _____

11. What was the date of sale? _____

12. What was the date of the first payment? _____

13. Are the payments on time? _____

14. What day of the month are the payments due? _____

15. Is there a balloon payment? _____

   (If so, how much and when is it due?) _____

16. What is the payor's credit score? _____

   16a. (If unknown ask: What does the payor do for a living?)

   _____

17. Have you received any other offers? _____

18. Is there anything else I should know about this note? _____

   _____

Also, it's common for the note holder not to remember all the details that you'll ask about – therefore get the answers to what you can and ask them to gather the rest and arrange another call.

If they have all the information you need, let the note holder know that you will be back in touch with them in a few days or as soon as you have an offer.

Remember, the only thing you have to focus on is finding out the note information, so when you list it on the website, the note buyer can give you an accurate price. From these bids, you will select the best offer, subtract

4%-8% for your finder's fee, and offer the remaining amount to the note seller. It's really simple, and we'll cover this in an upcoming chapter. Get excited, because in a few days from today you could be making more money than you ever dreamed possible!

Points to remember:

- If you can get the information about the note from a conversation, you have the potential to make a lot of money.

- Be sure to set up a follow up call with the note holder.

- Don't be concerned about not knowing enough. You now know more than 90% of the folks who have notes and the best way to overcome this concern is by doing your first deal.

A REAL ESTATE SECRET SUCCESS STORY

"To become involved in this business means financial freedom, independence, and not having to answer to someone everyday. I made $8,700.69 on my 1st deal."

- Student, Patty M., Florida

HIGH RESPONSE POSTCARDS

Strategy at a glance:

You mail out about 100 to 500 postcards at a time, depending on your time and budget.

Then the calls will start coming in, often out of pure curiosity.

At first, let your answering machine take the calls and ask the callers to leave their names, telephone numbers, and the reasons they are calling.

Remember:

Some people are calling out of curiosity and others are very serious. Treat both as strong potential deals whether you are working with them now or plan to follow up with them in the future.

Front:

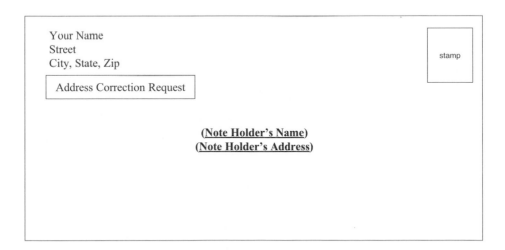

NOTE: A computer-generated mailing label is okay, but the more personalized you can make it the better.

Back:

> *I heard you've been collecting payments on a private loan or "note." I would love to give you cash right now so you don't have to worry about collecting payments anymore.*
>
> *Please call me at 1-800-555-1234 or visit my website at www.yourwebsite.com for a free, no obligation quote!*
>
> *Thank you,*
> *Russ*

NOTE: You may use a local phone number or an 800 number, either one works well. The key is to just make this easy and do it. In addition, please be sure to include your contact and website information.

> *I have been trying to contact you about Trust Deeds & Mortgages your clients hold.*
>
> *In fact, I have a report on how your clients can get the most for their note – It's a $29 value, Free!*
>
> *Call 1-800-555-1234 and we'll rush you a copy!*
>
> *Thank you,*
> *Russ*

The above are examples you can send to professionals and note holders to generate deals. You can use your own variation on the concept. I always like a "call to action," which means you tell the post card recipient to actually do something. You could try giving away a free report, a newsletter, an article that you create, or a free quote. This example is to get you thinking!

NOTE: Always send yourself a postcard whenever you do a mailing. By doing this, you can experience receiving one of your postcards and make sure the mailing went through. And always update the addresses that are returned to you from the post office so you can keep your list up to date.

NOTE ANALYSIS WORKSHEET

The NOTE ANALYSIS WORKSHEET can be used to organize the information you collected by following THE TELEPHONE SCRIPT on pages 157-158. Keep in mind that this worksheet has been designed for multiple types of notes, so you won't always have everything filled out.

Note Analysis Worksheet

Note Seller Name: _____ Date: _____

Address: _____ Phone #:_____

Property Information

Property Address: _____

Type of Property: _____ Owner Occupied?: _____

Sales Price: $_____ Date of Sale: _____

Property Value: $_____ Established By – Sale/Other: _____ Date: _____

1st loan Amount: $_____ Monthly Pmt: $_____ New / Assumed

2nd loan Amount: $_____ Monthly Pmt: $_____ New / Assumed

Down Pmt Amount: $_____ LTV: _____% ITV: _____%

Note Information

Original Amount: $_____ Balance: $_____ As of:_____

Interest Rate: _____% Payment Amount: $_____ Date of 1st Payment: _____

Original Length: _____ mos. Type: Amort, I/O, Other _____

Number of Payments Made: _____ Number Remaining:_____

Are the payments on time?: _____ What day of the month are they due?: _____

Balloon Payments (If any): $_____ Balloon payment due date: _____

Are there any clauses: _____

Seller Information

Note Seller's Motivation: _____

When Needs To Close: _____ Received other offers?: $_____

What does the Payor do for a living? _____

Payor's credit score: _____

Is there anything else I should know about this note?: _____

_____

NOTE ANALYSIS WORKSHEET EXAMPLE

Note Analysis Worksheet

Note Seller Name: _John Seller_   Date: _1/15/2009_

Address: _7233 Church Ranch Blvd.,_   Phone #: _1-800-620-6700_
Westminster, CO 80021

Property Information

Property Address: _124 Walnut St., Houston, TX 77001_

Type of Property: _SFR_   Owner Occupied?: _Yes_

Sales Price: $ _150,000_   Date of Sale: _7/8/2006_

Property Value: $ _150,000_ Established By – Sale/Other: _Sale_ Date: _7/8/2006_

1st loan Amount: $ _100,000_ Monthly Pmt: $ _805.59_ (New) Assumed

2nd loan Amount: $ _0_   Monthly Pmt: $ _N/A_ New / Assumed

Down Pmt Amount: $ _50,000_ LTV: _63_ % ITV: _____%

Note Information

Original Amount: $ _100,000_   Balance: $ _94,060.95_ As of: _1/15/2009_

Interest Rate: _7.5_ % Payment Amount: $ _805.59_ Date of 1st Payment: _8/1/2006_

Original Length: _240_   mos. Type: (Amort) I/O, Other _____

Number of Payments Made: _30_   Number Remaining: _210_

Are the payments on time?: _Yes_   What day of the month are they due?: _1st_

Balloon Payments (if any): $ _N/A_   Balloon payment due date: _N/A_

Are there any clauses: _5% late fee after the 10th of the month_

Seller Information

Note Seller's Motivation: _Reinvest_

When Needs To Close: _ASAP_   Received other offers?: $ _No_

What does the Payor do for a living? _Teacher_

Payor's credit score: _670_

Is there anything else I should know about this note?: _Great Payors!_

KEY TERMS FOR NOTE INVESTIGATION

Here is a description of a few key terms you will find on the NOTE ANALYSIS WORKSHEET.

Type of Property:

This describes the general category of the real estate securing the payment stream. "SFR" stands for Single Family Residence, and describes most free-standing homes with accompanying land included in the deal.

Payor's Credit:

The higher the credit score, the better, because the stronger the payor's credit rating, the better the odds that there won't be a problem with late payments or skipping out on obligations of the note entirely. From a note buyer's point of view, there's a lower risk of having to foreclose or become the owner of the property when the payor has a high credit score. Credit is one of the four key parameters we'll be using to grade notes with the Note Grading And Pricing Guidelines (NGPG) which you'll be learning about in Chapter 8 – Determining the Value of Real Estate IOUs.

Property Value:

This is simply the dollar figure claimed as the current value of the real estate securing the note. It will be important later to clarify whether or not this figure is based on something believable, such as a recent appraisal, or a tax assessment, or just a random figure that the note seller is claiming the house or property is worth. Property value is a critical piece of information because it determines the payor's equity, another one of the four factors used to grade notes according to NGPG.

Owner Occupied:

A property will either be owner occupied or non-owner occupied. If the property is owner occupied then that means the payor is actually living in the property, which is a good thing. Typically a payor has a stronger motivation to keep paying on the note when they live in the home, as opposed to a payor that lives some where else and rents the home out.

A property that is not owner occupied commonly implies that the property is being used to generate income. In other words, it's a rental property, possibly a condo, duplex, or summer/vacation home.

Keep in mind that an owner occupied property is preferred. Many buyers shy away from buying a note where the security property is vacant, or being renovated. An empty house raises the suspicion that the property isn't attractive, or maybe that it's not even fit for living in.

Sales Date:

This is the date that the real estate was sold. It is usually safe to assume that the date the note was created was close to the sales date (or that same day). This will be an important piece of information for gauging whether the information is accurate overall. For example, let's say the sales date is January 20, 2002, but the first note payment is listed as June 15, 2002. Immediately, you should be thinking "Why did almost six months pass before the first payment was made?"

And then ask the note seller why this is the case. If you don't understand something or it doesn't make sense always, always, always ask the appropriate question for the answer.

Down Payment:

This is the amount that the buyer of the property (the payor) put down at the time of sale; the down payment is money that the buyer puts directly towards the purchase of the property. The larger the down payment, the more assurance any potential note buyers will have in the reliability of the payor. This is because the down payment represents a cash figure that will be lost if the payor falls behind in their payments and the note holder forecloses. The down payment also creates equity in the property.

Face Value of the Note:

This is a very important number to understand. The face value of the note is the amount that was originally financed. For example, if the note is in first position you simply take the sales price, subtract the down payment and arrive at the face value of the note. The face value does NOT necessarily relate to what the note is actually worth to a buyer (that's the purchase price). And the face value is not what one still owes on the note (that's the note balance). It is the original amount that was borrowed and will never change.

Note Balance:

This is the current pay-off amount of the note. Let's say the payor wins the lottery, and calls up the note holder to say: "I want to pay off what I owe you in full – today." The note balance would be that amount.

Interest:

The annual interest rate the payor is obligated to pay. Interest causes the total amount paid to escalate over time. The longer it takes to pay off the note and the higher the interest rate, the more dollars the payor will actually pay over and above the initial face value of the note.

Many notes are amortized, which mean the monthly payment includes interest and principal. Some notes are interest-only meaning that the monthly payments are just enough to cover the interest payment on the note.

Payment Amount:

This is the dollar figure the payor is obligated to give to the note holder each month (or on each designated payment interval) to pay down their loan. With interest-only notes, the repeating payment will not actually reduce the debt. In these cases there will be a larger payment or payments in the future, called a "balloon payment."

When 1st Payment Made:

This date is typically about one month after the sales date and represents the day the 1st installment (payment) was made.

Next Payment Due Date:

For notes that are amortized monthly and current (up to date), this date should be one month from the last payment date.

Loan to Value (LTV):

LTV is the amount owed divided by the property value. From a buyer's perspective, the lower the LTV, the safer the note purchase.

Current or Delinquent:

This describes whether the payor is "up to date" on payments or "behind." Obviously, current is better. A delinquent status, however, does not mean that the note is not sellable. In fact, some buyers seek out notes that have a delinquent or non-performing status.

Balloon Payment, How Much Balloon Payment,
When Balloon Payment Due:

These three lines are for notes that have a future payment that pays some or all of the remaining balance. There MUST be a balloon payment for all interest-only notes, and on other notes that are not fully amortized.

Position of Note:

A note is typically in "first" or "second" position. While there are also third position notes, these are uncommon and harder to sell. First position means the loan was the first lien recorded against the property. "Firsts" are generally regarded as most secure by note buyers.

Remaining Balance:

This is the payoff amount of the note. You could be dealing with a 1st remaining balance or a 2nd remaining balance depending on the position of the note you are working with.

Contact Information:

This is the contact information of the person selling the note. This could be the note holder directly, or it could be a note finder – i.e., someone else who is looking to sell the note. It's important to find out who you're working with early in all of your note interviews.

Most of the note information is very self-explanatory. Having a good grasp on all of these basic pieces of the note information is a huge part of being effective – and successful. And, being able to sum up the notes you find in a logical and simple manner is something you'll quickly learn and then be able to communicate to the buyer of the note for great success.

A BLUEPRINT FOR YOUR NOTE BUSINESS

I often find that people get so excited about the incredible opportunities available to them through the note business that they often neglect to first sit down and define their plan which ultimately shapes their business. In fact, only 5% of business owners in the U.S. actually sit down and closely analyze their business philosophy and style. Isn't that remarkable? That's probably the reason so many businesses fail.

As a small business owner, you need to assess how you will work the business, how you will find customers, and how you will interact with these customers to meet their needs as well as your own.

Remember, gaining referrals through your target market is your number one goal!

Every business could use a careful evaluation from time to time. In order to help facilitate this evaluation process, I have made STEPS TO SUCCESS: A BLUEPRINT FOR YOUR NOTE BUSINESS available online at **www.notefindersresourcekit.com/blueprint**. The worksheet that you can receive at the website above will help you refine your marketing plan. Think of the questions on the worksheet as the building blocks you can use to create a fully functioning, highly successful business that is both rewarding and fulfilling.

The questions are designed specifically to give you an outline for thinking more critically about how you'll begin your new in-home business. Take the time to fill it out completely – you will find the insights you gain will be worth their weight in gold! Think carefully and deeply about your answers – assess yourself honestly.

One of my goals is to help you become the best seller financed real estate note finder that you can be. By spending the necessary time downloading and completing the worksheet, you'll be giving yourself the best opportunity for a quick start and ongoing success! You will be one of the few business people that have taken the time to thoroughly evaluate and think about your new business. Remember, the key to success is just staying excited until you get your first deal. After that, you'll never want to do anything else.

WHY SOPHISTICATED NOTE BUYERS ARE INTERESTED IN REAL ESTATE NOTES!

Here's an example from one of my first note deals:

In this example I am dealing with a $27,000 interest only balloon note. This means that the monthly payment is only enough to cover interest and there will be a balloon payment of the entire amount borrowed at the end of the term. To calculate what my yield is, I need to have 4 pieces of information as listed below.

On this specific note of $27,000, the "N" (term or length of the note) is 25 months, the "PV" (present value or offer in this case) is $14,800, the "PMT" (payment) is $202.50, the "FV" (future value or balloon amount here) is $27,000.

So I would input in the calculator the facts I know and then press the "I" or Interest Rate key to find out my yield!

In this example the buyer (me) is paying $14,800 now for a balloon payment of $27,000 due on the 25th month and after 24 monthly interest payments.

N	PV	PMT	FV
25	$14,800	$202.50	$27,000

YIELD

41.8%

THE TOTAL RETURN IS 41.8% PER YEAR

When I first started doing this the only way to make money with real estate notes was to buy them, which could be risky. Over the years I perfected this system so that all you have to do to make incredible money is find them!

* **NOTE**: *The above example requires the use of a financial calculator. One popular financial calculator you can use is the Hewlett Packard 10BII.*

A REAL ESTATE SECRET SUCCESS STORY

"With the money back guarantee I knew I didn't have much to lose... you're not going to know unless you try, and if I can do it, anybody can do it. I've made $22,430.00 so far."

- Student, Mark S., Wisconsin

How to Make Money Working with Real Estate IOUs

GETTING STARTED AS A NOTE FINDER

Spend a few hours a week following my plan – you can see results quickly and easily.

1. Gather a list of 500 note holders to contact via mail.

2. Gather a list of 500 professionals who may know of notes that are available for sale. Attorneys, CPAs, Title Agents, Real Estate Agents, and Mortgage Brokers, and other professionals (I've provided a list on page 133).

Getting your target lists:

1. To find note holders, I recommend going to your local courthouse and looking up "mortgagees" or you can save hours of time by using *Finding IOUs Easy.* There you'll find millions and millions of dollars in notes right in your own back yard. This is your target market that you will want to send a postcard or letter every 6 to 8 weeks. Don't change your target list because repetition is the key to this market! Changing lists is where new students make their mistake. If you don't see an immediate response don't be alarmed or get frustrated simply mail to the list again and again. I've seen this technique work over and over and it can work for you too, so long as you stick with it.

2. To find professional note sources (Attorneys, CPAs, Mortgage Brokers and Real Estate Agents), you can either look in your phone book or call a local list broker for those names. You may find list brokers in your local phone book under "mailing services." Keep in mind, your goal is to have ten professionals telling you about notes that are available for sale. If you have ten professionals referring notes to you each year you could earn a nice income.

3. Remember, the key to marketing is repetition and follow up. In fact, I have found that when someone sees your name in print five times, they feel as if they know you, even if they have never met

you! This is a marketing tactic that all good marketers know and understand. Your success comes from marketing yourself and your services over and over to the same audience.

Many of my marketing secrets won't cost you a dime to implement. Some, like sending out a postcard, will cost you a few pennies, but will have the potential to return thousands and thousands of dollars every time you do. Remember, if you are not marketing your business, then you are not in business! Marketing, which simply means effectively getting the word out about what you do, is the key to success in any business.

And, it's even possible to automate the whole process so that all you are doing is answering the phone. This is the greatest business in the world because it is possible to build a substantial income working in your spare time.

Professional image building tools:

Here are a few tools you can use to build your image and business to provide you with an income of your dreams:

Business cards, a brochure, a newsletter, a website, and email.

Personally, I believe that utilizing all of the above tools is the very best way to go for the fastest result possible. My favorite way to locate notes for sale is by sending out your own personalized newsletter. You can receive a lot of ideas and information about how to create your own personal newsletter at our website. I will give you the web address and other reference materials later on in the book.

A specific plan of action:

1. Write down what you would like to achieve in this business.

2. Get a list of your target note sources.

3. Mail to your target note sources every 6 to 8 weeks.

4. Turbo-charge your results by following up with calls to your note sources. If you don't like doing the calls yourself, you can hire a local college student to do them for you. Sample calling scripts and example phone situations are available online at **www.notefindersresourcekit.com**. They are short, casual, and friendly. And of course, you don't have to call to make money at this. It's simply a suggestion for those who want to take this business all the way and earn a lot of money.

The goal is to simply develop a relationship with your note sources as they could refer business in the future. It's simple, fun and will never feel like you are "selling" because you're not. What you're doing is offering someone money for something they didn't really want in the first place. It's a nice way to create a business and it's a win-win for everyone involved!

THE 30 BEST WAYS TO FIND NOTES

It is important to remember, when looking for notes, that massive action produces massive results. You're about to learn several ways to make money with seller financed notes. If you use several methods at one time, you could see great results very fast. Try a few different strategies and see which method best suits your strengths. Since some methods are bound to work better than others, you should focus on those areas specifically that work best for you and suit your personality. Often the effectiveness of strategies differs based on geographical location, population demographic, and other circumstances.

Some of my students feel the following are issues they face and all can be easily remedied as you'll see:

- **Lack** of **credibility**

- **Lack** of **deals** crossing your desk

- **Lack** of **experience** and **confidence**

By having many notes come across your desk each day you will solve all of these perceived issues on the list above. So how do you do this? You are about to learn over 30 ways to have notes find you so you have a consistent supply of notes coming to you all the time and I'll even show you a few of my personal favorites.

When it comes to marketing, it is very important to remember: I said it before and I'll say it again because it's so important – if someone sees your name in print five times they feel as if they know you, even if they've never met you. So, the key to successful marketing as a note finder, is repetition. Repetition to the same group of people will be your biggest key to success.

You should market to two main groups:

1. Note holders

2. Referral sources (Professionals who encounter clients with notes)

Marketing to note holders:

Marketing directly to note holders can be profitable, but you have to remember – it's most likely a one-shot deal. In other words, you find a note holder, submit their note, and find them a buyer. The deal is done, and while you make a quick and easy profit, that resource has been fully exhausted (in most cases) because most note holders have just one note. However, this is a very fast way to receive deals, even though it could cost you a little money. If I had known what I'm telling you now when I started this business back in 1990, I would have saved tens of thousands of dollars.

Marketing to referral sources:

Marketing to referral sources does not produce results as quickly as marketing directly to note holders, but over time, it is much more cost effective. It may take you time to get a good referral source, but that one good source could potentially refer many deals to you year after year. So, by marketing both to note holders and referral sources, you will immediately have note deals to work on as well as a renewable source of note deals for the future, which is very exciting.

Keep these ideas in mind:

- You have found a company that truly cares about your financial success. My staff and I will help you succeed. I challenge you to find a staff that is more committed to your success.

- Never give up! The only way you can fail is if you quit. Please remember this.

- This is an "earn as you learn" business. Make money while applying what you learn and remember, you don't have to master everything in this book to get started.

These are the ways to get answers to any questions you may have immediately:

- Send us an **email** at **support@dalbeyeducation.com**. This is probably the best way for us to give you the help you need

- **FAQ Section** – We have created an extensive list of the most commonly asked questions.
  Go to **www.notenetwork.com/members/FAQ.php3** and you will find the answers to the questions we hear the most..

THE 30 BEST WAYS TO MARKET YOUR NOTE BUSINESS

I would like to break up "The 30 Best Ways to Market Your Note Business" into two sections: The people you can market to, and the methods you could use to market yourself.

These are professionals who could become referral sources for your business:

- Appraisers
- Attorneys
- Bail Bondsperson
- Builders
- CPAs
- Collection Agencies

- Contractors
- Developers
- FSBO Ads*
- Financial Planners
- Loan Service Cos.
- Mortgage Brokers

- Nursing Homes
- Property Mgmt. Cos.
- Real Estate Agents
- Retirement Communities
- Title & Escrow Officers

*FSBO means "For Sale By Owner"

These are methods to market your business:

- Business Cards
- Courthouse
- Email
- Internet
- Newsletters

- Newspaper Ads
- Postcards
- Postcard Decks
- Radio
- Seminars

- Telemarketing
- Word of Mouth
- Write Articles

WHO TO FOCUS ON AND HOW TO GET THEIR BUSINESS

Appraisers:

Appraisers place values on real estate properties. They may know of notes that have been created on properties. Locate appraisers in the Yellow Pages. **Marketing:** Send them a postcard, newsletter, or business card telling them what you do and follow up with a telephone call.

Attorneys:

Attorneys are great sources of note leads. Most people overlook attorneys as referral sources, but believe me – they come across *more* notes than some real estate agents. This is one of the best groups to market to. **Marketing:** The best way to get attorneys to refer business to you is to offer them a free informational newsletter describing the services you offer. Remember, everyone loves and is interested in real estate. You might not get through to them with letters, postcards or phone calls. An informational newsletter is a better way to capture their attention.

Bail Bondsperson:

A bail bondsperson is someone who puts up bail for people in jail. A bail bondsperson will often secure his/her investment by creating a note secured by real estate. Many bail bondspeople have lots of notes for sale. Again, they are easy to locate in your Yellow Pages. **Marketing:** You can market to bail bondspeople using letters, postcards, telemarketing, newsletters, or a personal visit to his/her office. One of the most effective ways to market to bail bondspeople is to mail a brochure or informational letter and then give them a follow up telephone call.

Builders:

Builders are often a good source of notes. Many times, they hold notes to facilitate a real estate sale. In most instances, builders need cash to complete their projects; therefore, they cannot have their money tied up in notes for long. A word of caution however, builders take small down payments and carry the majority of the balance in the form of a note. If there is a small down payment, the note buyer will want a significantly higher discount on the note. The reason for this is that the buyer of the property will not have much to lose and could easily walk away from their obligation to pay if they have only a small down payment in the property. **Marketing:** The two most effective ways to reach builders are telemarketing and direct mail. In order to find builders in your area, look for a local builders association who can provide you a list or look in your phone book to start your own list.

CPAs:

Certified public accountants, bookkeepers and financial planners are other excellent sources of notes. Of all referral sources, I rank CPAs as number two (attorneys being number one) as the best individuals for referrals. They work with a variety of people and their clients often need to liquidate a real estate note. **Marketing:** One potential way to reach CPAs is to use direct mail and follow-up phone calls. One of the most effective direct mail methods is to send a personalized newsletter every quarter (four times a year) and a follow-up postcard six weeks later (four times a year).

Collection Agencies:

Collection agencies can be great sources of notes. Frequently, collection agencies collect from people who have real estate investments. You will be surprised at how often you find debtors carrying real estate notes. Again, look them up in your local phone book. **Marketing:** First call these companies to make a personal contact and tell them what you do: "I help people who are collecting payments secured by real estate to get cash now." Next, follow up with a personal letter as well as newsletter and postcard reminders every six weeks.

Contractors:

Contractors are much like builders – they may be forced to carry back notes on completed projects. **Marketing:** Like builders, the two most effective ways to reach contractors – telemarketing and direct mail. Look in your area for a contractor association. Often, you can purchase lists of contractors with a contact name, address and phone number. Otherwise, look in your phone book for contact information. I will go into more detail on telemarketing and direct mail later in this book.

Developers:

Developers purchase land to build developments on. It is common for developers to carry back notes in order to sell individual properties that they build. Developers are like builders, only on a much larger scale. There are three levels of developers: small developers, medium-sized developers, and large developers. Generally, developers most in need of money are small-sized companies; therefore, the best deals will be from these developers. **Marketing:** Again, the best ways to reach developers: telemarketing and direct mail. Look in your area for a developer association – you can often purchase a list with contact information. Otherwise, look in your phone book for this.

FSBO Ads:

FSBO means For Sale By Owner. In many areas there are small newspapers that focus on FSBO properties. **Marketing:** Call the sellers and explain seller financing and ultimately how you can get them their cash. Send the seller your newsletter – nothing will impress him/her more than to receive an informational newsletter about real estate.

Financial Planners:

Financial planners know all about their clients' financial affairs, and are therefore good sources of referrals. You can find financial planners in your local phone book. **Marketing:** When marketing to financial planners, send them a newsletter or brochure in the mail and follow up with a phone call.

Loan Servicing Companies:

A loan servicing company collects payments on notes for note holders. In other words, the person who is collecting the payments chooses to have a company manage the collecting process, because the person receiving the monthly payments doesn't want the added hassle involved. **Marketing:** Contact these companies and ask them if you may include a flyer or brochure with the statements they send out. Most loan servicing companies send out monthly statements updating account information to the mortgagee or the note holder. This is an excellent opportunity for you to get in front of the note holder – the one receiving the monthly payments.

Mortgage Brokers:

Mortgage brokers create traditional loans on real estate. They can be an excellent source of referrals because they run across people who need money to purchase property. Some of them are holding notes and you could help them get the cash they need. You can refer people to the mortgage broker and the mortgage broker can refer people to you. **Marketing:** Mortgage brokers are easy to find – just look in your local phone book. Contact them via the phone or through direct mail.

Nursing Homes:

Often when people move into a nursing home, they have to liquidate all of their assets. **Marketing:** Contact nursing homes in your area and explain your services. They will be happy to hear from you. Also, arrange to go to the nursing home to make a presentation about what you do. This could be an excellent source of referrals for you. Contact nursing homes via the telephone and direct mail.

Property Management:

Property management companies manage properties for their owners. It is common for these owners to have notes on property and, if they knew about your services, it is likely they'd be interested in selling their notes. **Marketing:** Find a list of property management companies in your local phone book. Contact them using direct mail and telemarketing.

Real Estate Agents:

Real estate agents can be a great source for note referrals. However, you may need to educate them about seller financing. Some realtors carry back their commissions when selling a property and may know of other realtors that have notes. **Marketing:** There are a few ways to market to realtors. Giving a presentation is one way to market to realtors. Call and make an appointment (Tuesdays are usually a good day) to present to realtors in their office. Remember, when you make a presentation, always bring something to eat like donuts or sandwiches. Mailing a brochure with a business card attached or an informational newsletter with your contact information on it is another way to reach realtors.

Retirement Communities:

Many large retirement communities have their own newspaper or newsletter. You also might consider marketing to retired people and their families, as they may have notes that they no longer care to own. **Marketing:** Place a small advertisement in these internal publications for minimal cost.

Title Officers and Escrow Officers:

In many states, title officers handle closings on property sales and make their money when the deal closes. Escrow officers put together real estate transactions; they are the ones who do all the paperwork (for the sake of clarity, in some states title companies facilitate these transactions). Often, title and escrow officers are involved in deals when seller financed notes are created. And remember: Nine times out of ten, when somebody sells real estate, they want their cash in-hand. Therefore, title and escrow officers would be happy to know about your services. **Marketing:** You can meet both of these groups in person. During this meeting explain what you do ("I help people sell notes for a lump sum of cash"). Be sure to leave a business card and either a brochure or a newsletter with your contact information on it. You may even ask if you can leave brochures or newsletters in their waiting area. You can purchase an acrylic rack for about $5.00 to place your brochures or newsletters in. You can also market to title officers using direct mail or telemarketing.

SIMPLE MARKETING METHODS

Business Cards:

There are many things you can do with your business cards. For example, you can insert your business card with every bill that you pay. If you are paying your telephone bill, insert your card. Your card might say, "I help sell notes, trust deeds and mortgages." Another way to market with your business card is to stick it on local bulletin boards located in your grocery store, coffee shop, realtor office, etc. And of course, you can give them out to referral sources and anyone you meet.

Courthouse:

Remember, every note secured by real estate is recorded at the local county courthouse. The courthouse has names and addresses of mortgagees. A mortgagee is a seller of a property who receives the monthly payments and holds the mortgage contract as security. In other words, it's the person you want to contact about their note. Go to your local courthouse and look up property sellers or mortgagees who have carried back the note. You will get a list of mortgagees that you can market to over and over. The best way to accomplish this is to send them a postcard. A postcard is what I call "mail they always read." Send them a postcard once every six to eight weeks (see a postcard example on pages 115-116). The key to postcard marketing is to make the postcard look personalized. Use a stamp and make your message look like it was handwritten.

A few large data mining companies have compiled information on mortgagees from many states and counties. In other words, they do the time consuming work and then sell lists of mortgagees to any interested party. In fact, it is not uncommon for these companies to sell their lists multiple times per year! So, if you do plan to purchase lists, be aware that you may run into additional competition.

With the above in mind, looking up names and addresses on your own takes time. When gathering names and addresses of note holders from the courthouse you can expect to find ten to fifteen leads per hour, but it could be a list that no one else has, ultimately providing an advantage.

This will be a great list for you, but it will take time to accumulate. You might want to hire a local college student to go to the courthouse for you. This can be an inexpensive way for you to accumulate a list that is truly yours.

Email:
In the new "information age," it's important to have your own email address as well as to build a contact list of potential note sellers and note referrals email addresses. Be sure to put your email address on all marketing pieces (business cards, newsletters, postcards, newspaper articles, etc.) so that people can contact you online any time, any day. As people begin to email you, you should keep track of these contacts and build a list of people to whom you can contact via email. There is a range of email marketing you can implement, from occasional informational emails to weekly reminders of your business name and services.

Internet:
Marketing on the Internet can be very tricky. There are literally millions of your potential customers on the Internet. The problem is that it's quite difficult for your target group to find you. The best way to market on the Internet is to have a professional looking website and then research methods to bring traffic to your site. Not only do you want traffic, you want the right kind of traffic.

If you do not have a professionally designed website with articles about the seller financed note business, you can obtain one very easily. I will give you more information about this later on in the book. Remember, the Internet is used primarily for one purpose – finding information. Also, you should always include your website in all email correspondence; this way your customers can simply click on the link and find out everything about your services in the note industry. Giving out good, high quality information is your key to becoming successful on the Internet.

Newsletters:

There's no better way for you to obtain credibility than to have your own personalized newsletter. The best part is that the entire newsletter marketing process can be automated. A mailing house can mail out your newsletters. All that is left for you to do is to answer the phone.

This is what you want – little time involvement with high profit potential. The more newsletters that you mail, the more money you could make.

Newspaper Ads:

Most note finders place newspaper ads when they get started however, their commitment to running an ad is not long enough to make it worthwhile. Newspaper ads can be good if you look for little niche newspapers in your area, but you may want to avoid big newspapers like the *LA Times*, the *Wall Street Journal* or *USA Today* because they are not very cost effective. Place small ads in many small newspapers. Your ad can read, "Cash for your trust deed or mortgage. Private party, call XXX-XXX-XXXX." Believe it or not, this ad is one of the best I've found.

You may also want to write a short article for some of these newspapers. It can be an article without pay, in exchange for exposure. At the end of each of your articles, say something like, "To subscribe to my newsletter or email on real estate, a $29.00 value, free, call XXX-XXX-XXXX." Have a voice mail message attached to that phone number instructing callers to leave their name, address, email address and phone number in order to receive your newsletter. This could save you a lot of time, and we all know – time is money. You want to capture all of this information so that you can continually market to this group of people who might refer notes to you in the future.

Postcards:

Postcard marketing is used mainly to remind people about what you do. It can also be used to market directly to note holders. It's an inexpensive way to put your message into the hands of potential customers. The key to postcard marketing is to make the postcard appear personalized.

Accomplish this by placing a stamp on the card and make your message look handwritten. Do this by writing your message on a postcard and take that card to your local printer – they can print thousands of them for next to nothing. Have it printed in blue ink to make it look personalized. If marketing to note holders, use a message like the one in the example of the high response postcard on pages 115-116.

Radio:

You can use radio to find notes in two ways. The first way is to advertise during specific real estate shows. In other words, you can have a 30-second ad telling listeners, "Cash for your trust deed or mortgage. Private party, call XXX-XXX-XXXX." or, something catchy to grab your audience's attention. Another great way to use radio is to be a guest host discussing real estate and seller financing. There are many radio stations that have talk shows about real estate and they always need people who can speak intelligently about the subject. This is an excellent way to gain credibility, exposure, and note deals. And at the end of your presentation simply tell the listeners that you'd be happy to send them a free copy of your newsletter if they call XXX-XXX-XXXX.

Seminars:

This is a great way to find notes for sale. Hold a seminar in your area – teach the concept of real estate notes. Advertise in newspapers or hook up with your local "Learning Annex" to reach potential attendees. Conduct a short one or two hour class and get the word out about what you do for free.

Telemarketing:

Telemarketing to note holders is one of the most overlooked ways to market your note business. I started calling note holders back in 1993, and on my first day, about four hours into it, I found an incredible deal. Telemarketing is a gold mine! Many people are afraid of the telephone (boy, I know I was), but the telephone can become your best friend. Every time you pick up the phone and make a call you could make money.

Telemarketing is a numbers game – the more calls you make the more possible deals you could have! But remember, just because you dial the phone a hundred times doesn't mean that you've talked with a hundred people. And even if it took you 20 hours or so to get your first potential deal, but you could make $3,600 for this one deal that's still a great hourly wage.

Now, what if you don't like making these calls yourself? Hire a local college student to call for you and find someone who is interested in selling their note.. If the deal closes, give a small bonus to your college helper. Don't overlook the power of telemarketing!

If you are planning on calling note holders directly or anyone you haven't spoken to before, be sure to check those names against the national Do-Not-Call registry. It's really easy to do and some states also maintain a Do-Not-Call list or registry. Telemarketers are required to search the National Do-Not-Call Registry at least once every 31 days and must not call the consumers registered on this list. To do this, you must also register yourself or your organization with the registry.

To access the registry, go to **www.telemarketing.donotcall.gov**. This is a secure government-regulated website.

Here you must set up a profile for yourself by providing information about yourself or your organization.

Please visit this website for more information:
http://www.ftc.gov/bcp/edu/pubs/business/alerts/alt129.htm

Word of Mouth:
Tell everyone you meet, everywhere you go, that you can help them, or anyone they know, sell their note. You can also join your local Chamber of Commerce and attend their meetings. Pass out business cards, brochures and newsletters. Before long, many people could be referring notes to you.

Remember, there are many, many different ways you can find seller financed real estate notes. Please don't feel like you have to do all of them to be successful because nothing is further from the truth. I've included these ways in the book to get your ideas flowing. Pick the one or two that best suit your personality and jump in. The truth is there are more notes out there than any of us could ever buy and these note holders need help getting them what they want and need – cash.

MY NINE FAVORITE MARKETING TECHNIQUES

I'm frequently asked, "Russ, what's the best, most effective way for me to market?" These are the ways I like to market for notes, with number 1 being my favorite:

1. Newsletter marketing

2. Telemarketing to note holders

3. Referrals from local professionals

    a. Attorneys

    b. CPAs

    c. Realtors

    d. Title and Escrow Officers

    e. Loan servicing companies

4. Internet marketing

Personally, I like the above methods the best because they are more proactive, but all methods are good and each one works. Pick the techniques that best suit your personality.

5. Courthouse records

6. Newspaper

7. Postcards

8. Voice mail

9. Letters

It's important to note that some marketing techniques carry a higher cost, but require less time, while others require a bit more time but at a lower cost. No matter which way you are inclined to go, please remember – we are here to support you 100%.

I have shared 30 of the very best ways I've found for you to market your note business and I've gone over my nine favorite marketing techniques. It's true that there are hundreds of different ways you can do this business, but I've pulled together the best of the best. My intention is to help you be efficient and successful – as quickly as possible.

Allow these ideas to percolate in your mind, and I'm sure you could come up with some additional ones. You don't have to reinvent the wheel. The wheel has already been created for you. Just follow my simple step-by-step plan and you could be successful too!

The real key to success is simple: Get out there and start talking to people. You don't have to know all of this stuff to start making money. I have so many students making millions combined and it's important for you to understand that they don't know everything about this business.

This is the greatest business in the world. And once you do your first deal you'll never want to do anything else again because it's so much fun.

The Note Finder Resource Kit

This section will teach you to build your business from the ground up, starting with a solid foundation.

Over the next few pages, I describe 7 tools that will become an important part of your daily note business. These tools are:

1. Note Analysis Worksheet

2. Commitment Letter – Send To Seller

3. Cover Letter To The Commitment Letter – Send To Seller

4. Information Request Form – Send To Seller

5. Non-Circumvent Agreement – Send To Buyer

6. Payout Agreement – Send To Buyer

7. Telephone Scripts

Please note: *Neither Russ Dalbey or his employees are giving legal advice or recommending you use these documents. These sample documents are provided to you for educational purposes only.*

All of these tools are included in the Note Finders Resource Kit. To receive your Note Finders Resource Kit simply go to: **www.notefindersresourcekit.com**

NOTE ANALYSIS WORKSHEET

The NOTE ANALYSIS WORKSHEET can be used to organize your information from the note holder interview. This worksheet has been designed for multiple types of notes and may include information that does not apply to every deal you work on. Remember, You can get a copy of this document in a Microsoft Word format by going to **www.notefindersresourcekit.com**.

If you follow the script on page 157-158 you will have all the information necessary to submit the note online at:

www.notenetwork.com/Noteservice.

Note Analysis Worksheet

Note Seller Name: _____ Date: _____

Address: _____ Phone #: _____

Property Information

Property Address: _____

Type of Property: _____ Owner Occupied?: _____

Sales Price: $_____ Date of Sale: _____

Property Value: $_____ Established By – Sale/Other: _____ Date: _____

1st loan Amount: $_____ Monthly Pmt: $_____ New / Assumed

2nd loan Amount: $_____ Monthly Pmt: $_____ New / Assumed

Down Pmt Amount: $_____ LTV: _____% ITV: _____%

Note Information

Original Amount: $_____ Balance: $_____ As of: _____

Interest Rate: _____% Payment Amount: $_____ Date of 1st Payment: _____

Original Length: _____ mos. Type: Amort, I/O, Other _____

Number of Payments Made: _____ Number Remaining: _____

Are the payments on time?: _____ What day of the month are they due?: _____

Balloon Payments (if any): $_____ Balloon payment due date: _____

Are there any clauses: _____

Seller Information

Note Seller's Motivation: _____

When Needs To Close: _____ Received other offers?: $_____

What does the Payor do for a living? _____

Payor's credit score: _____

Is there anything else I should know about this note?: _____

_____

COMMITMENT LETTER
Send To Seller

The COMMITMENT LETTER is a simple contract that you will send the seller of the note as soon you have agreed upon a price. This letter will commit the seller and take the note off the market. If the seller cancels the agreement, then they are obligated to reimburse you $125 for your time and any expenses that may have occurred. Yes, you make $125 even if they say, "No." This is located on the next page – the 2nd to last paragraph. Notice that if you or your buyer cancels the agreement, for any reason, you may cancel your agreement with the seller without penalty to you. The COMMITMENT LETTER obligates the seller, not you or the buyer(s).

THIS COMMITMENT TO BUY, is made **(Date)** by and between **(Seller's Name)**, the undersigned (Seller), and **(Your Name)**, (Buyer), and/or its successors and assigns, whose address is **(Your Address)**.

This commitment is made in **(Your County)** county, subject to and contingent upon **(Your Name)**, and/or its buyer's inspection and approval of the property and all documents including, but not limited to, credit, appraisal and title work.

Seller agrees to sell and convey to Buyer, and Buyer agrees to buy, upon the terms and conditions set herein, that certain **(Trust Deed, Mortgage, Land Contract, or Other Named Security Instrument)** wherein the Payor owes a current principal balance of **($ Principal Balance)** as of this month, carrying interest on the principal balance at the rate of **(Interest Rate %)** per annum, and requiring a monthly payment of **($ Monthly Payment)**.

The agreed purchase price is the sum of **($ Purchase Price)** provided there are no underlying problems. If the contract has to be renegotiated a verbal commitment from the seller will be binding.

The subject property is located in **(County Property is Located In)** County and is legally described as follows; **(Property Address)**

ADDITIONAL LEGAL DESCRIPTION TO BE PROVIDED AND VERIFIED BEFORE CLOSING

Seller warrants that:

1. There are no prior liens or encumbrances on the property subject to the Instrument except as stated below:

SUBJECT TO: **(Other Liens or Encumbrances)**

2. It has full power, authority and legal right to execute, deliver, and perform, its obligation under this letter;

3. This Letter and the Instrument are legally valid and binding, and enforceable in accordance with their terms, and there are no claims or defenses, personal or otherwise, or offsets whatsoever to the enforceability or validity of the Instrument;

4. There are no lawsuits or legal proceedings pending, or to the best of Seller's knowledge, threaten regarding encumbrances on, or the ownership, use or possession of, the property or the Instrument;

5. No brokerage or other commission is due and unpaid in connection with the Instrument; and,

6. Seller has, as of the date of this letter, and will have as of the date of the closing, good, marketable title to the Instrument.

During our processing period any additional payments made to Seller on the Instrument which reduce the principal balance by an amount equal to or greater than one hundred dollars ($100) will also cause a minor adjustment in the purchase price at closing.

Seller agrees to return any payments received after the closing of this Instrument.

Seller understands that **(Your Name)**, is not acting as an advisor for Seller in connection with this transaction, nor as Seller's agent, but rather is dealing with Seller at arms length, at all times.

Seller acknowledges that it has sought and received whatever independent legal, tax, accounting or other advice it desires concerning this transaction. Further, Seller is not relying on **(Your Name)**, in entering into this transaction, but is acting on their own best judgment.

Seller agrees to execute all necessary documents to effect the assignment and conveyance to Buyer of its interest in the Instrument. Seller agrees to furnish any and all documents in its possession necessary to consummate this transaction. If, after closing, it is discovered that errors, omissions, or loss of documents has occurred, Seller agrees to cooperate with the Buyer to correct any and all errors, omissions, or losses within ten (10) days of receipt of notice from Buyer.

Upon our receipt of all the necessary closing documents related to this transaction, we should be able to close within thirty (30) to forty-five (45) days.

All normal closing costs will be the responsibility of the Buyer with the exception of any additional, or unexpected, legal cost necessary to clear or perfect title.

Should the Seller fail to close, after signing this agreement, Seller shall be obligated to reimburse Buyer for all out-of-pocket expenses incurred related to this transaction, up to the time of cancellation. These expenses should normally be limited to title and/or appraisal fees, plus the processing fee of one hundred and twenty-five dollars ($125.00).

Buyer hereby gives Seller a specific period of three days to complete, and return, this Commitment Letter, and agrees to keep this offer open for that period of time. If Seller is unable to complete, and return this agreement within the allotted time, this agreement shall be canceled. Buyer may extend the time period, upon conditions it deems acceptable.

_____   _____   _____
  (Your Signature)   **(Your Printed Name)**   **(Date)**

_____   _____   _____
 (Seller's Signature)   **(Seller's Printed Name)**   **(Date)**

COVER LETTER TO THE COMMITMENT LETTER
Send To Seller

(Today's Date)
(Seller's Name)
(Seller's Street)
(Seller's City, State, Zip)

Dear **(Seller's Name)**,

Thank you for the opportunity to be of service to you. We will do everything possible to expedite your closing once you return the enclosed "Information Request Form" and copies of the requested documents.

The cash you will receive is **($ Purchase Price)** for the full sale of your note, which has **(Number of Remaining Payments)** remaining payments.

A typical transaction takes thirty (30) to forty-five (45) days to process, provided there are no unusual circumstances that arise. The normal closing process includes a credit evaluation on the payor, a drive-by appraisal and a title policy review. We pay for all of the normal closing costs.

Occasionally, purchases have to be renegotiated or canceled if the review process reveals underlying problems that cannot be corrected. Thankfully, this situation doesn't happen very often. If it does, you retain the right to cancel the transaction without any obligation on your part.

Also, enclosed is a formal "Commitment Letter" which begins the closing process and states our obligation to you. Please sign it and return it with the above requested documents. Call us if you have questions or want more information.

Sincerely,

(Your Signature)
(Your Printed Name)
(Your Contact Information)

INFORMATION REQUEST FORM
Send To Seller

The INFORMATION REQUEST FORM indicates the documents and information that you will want the note seller to send to you. You want to send this form to the seller along with the COMMITMENT LETTER and COVER LETTER TO THE COMMITMENT LETTER.

(Today's Date)
(Seller's Name)
(Seller's Street)
(Seller's City, State, Zip)

INFORMATION FOR NOTE SALE

Dear **(Seller's Name)**,

Please send the documents listed below to me at the address given below.

_____ Copy of Note
_____ Copy of Trust Deed, Mortgage, or Land Contract
_____ Escrow instructions and closing statement from real estate
        sale in which the Trust Deed was created
_____ Title insurance policy which insures the Trust Deed
_____ Fire insurance information on the property which secures
        the Trust Deed (Insurance Company, Policy Number,
        Agent's Name and Address)
_____ Loan Payment Record
_____ If available most recent appraisal and credit report

Please check off the above items when assembled and mail to me at **(Your Address)**. If you have any questions, you may call me at **(Your Telephone Number)**.

Thank you,
(Your Signature)
(Your Printed Name)
(Your Contact Information)

NON-CIRCUMVENT AGREEMENT
Send To Buyer

The NON-CIRCUMVENT AGREEMENT is designed to protect your interest when you are finding notes and referring them to buyers. As you know, you will have a fee due to you for referring the note to the buyer and this document will protect you. Normally, you'll find buyers to do exactly what they say they will do, however, this document just gives you more assurance.

NON-CIRCUMVENTION,   NON-DISCLOSURE   AND CONFIDENTIALITY AGREEMENT

THIS AGREEMENT entered into on this **(Day)** day of **(Month)**, **(Year)** is for the Professional Association and arrangement of Non-Circumvention, Non-Disclosure and Confidentiality between **(Your Name)** whose office is at **(Your Address)** and **(Buyer's Name)** whose principal place of business is at **(Buyer's Address)** hereinafter, called the "The Parties." The Parties with this agree to respect the integrity and tangible value of this agreement between them.

THIS AGREEMENT is a perpetuating guarantee for five (5) years from the date of execution and is to be applied to any and all transactions present and future, of the introducing party, including subsequent follow-up, repeat, extended, renegotiated, and new transactions regardless of the success of the project.

Because of THIS AGREEMENT, the Parties involved in this transaction may learn from one another, or from principals, the names and telephone numbers of note buyers, borrowers, lenders, agents, finders, banks, lending corporations, individuals and/or trusts, or Buyers and Sellers hereinafter called contacts. The Parties with this acknowledge, accept and agree that the identities of the contacts will be recognized by the other Party as exclusive and valuable contacts of the introducing Party and will remain so for the duration of this agreement.

The Parties agree to keep confidential the names of any contacts introduced or revealed to the other party, and that their firm, company, associates, corporations, joint ventures, partnerships, divisions, subsidiaries, employees, agents, heirs, assigns, designees, or consultants will not contact, deal with, negotiate or participate in any transactions with any of the contacts without first entering a written agreement with the Party who provided such contact unless that Party gives prior written permission. Such confidentiality will include any names, addresses, telephone numbers, facsimile numbers, email addresses and/or other pertinent information disclosed or revealed to either Party.

The Parties agree not to disclose, reveal or make use of any information during discussion or observation regarding methods, concepts, ideas, product/services, or proposed new products or services, nor to do business with any of the revealed contacts without the written consent of the introducing party or parties.

The Parties agree that due to the many variables surrounding each Business/ Financial Transaction that will occur because of this agreement, the commission to be paid and/or the fee structure between the Parties can vary. A separate pay out agreement is attached here to outline compensation for each Business/Financial Transaction. The pay out agreement must be drafted and acknowledged by signature before all Business/Financial Transactions.

In case of circumvention, the Parties agree and guarantee that they will pay a legal monetary penalty that is equal to the commission or fee the circumvented Party should have realized in such transactions, by the person(s) engaged on the circumvention for each occurrence. If either party commences legal proceedings to interpret or enforce the terms of THIS AGREEMENT, the prevailing Party will be entitled to recover court costs and reasonable attorney fees.

The parties will construe THIS AGREEMENT in accordance with the laws of the State of **(Your State)**, County of **(Your County)**. If any provision of this agreement is found to be void by any court of competent jurisdiction, the remaining provisions will remain in force and effect.

THIS AGREEMENT contains the entire understanding between the Parties and any waiver, amendment or modification to THIS AGREEMENT will be subject to the above conditions and must be attached hereto.

Upon execution of THIS AGREEMENT by signature below, the Parties agree that any individual, firm company, associates, corporations, joint ventures, partnerships, divisions, subsidiaries, employees, agents, heirs, assigns, designees or consultants of which the signee is an agent, officer, heir, successor, assign or designee is bound by the terms of THIS AGREEMENT.

A facsimile copy of this Non-Circumvention, Non-Disclosure and Confidentiality Agreement shall constitute a legal and binding instrument. By setting forth my hand below I warrant that I have complete authority to enter into THIS AGREEMENT.

For: **(Buyer's Company Name)**

(Buyer's Signature)   (Buyer's Printed Name)   (Date)

(Note Finder's Signature)   (Note Finder's Printed Name)   (Date)

If you would like additional lists of documents for closing and managing your own personal transactions, I recommend that you go to the link below for more information:

www.notenetwork.com/helptips

Keep in mind, the sample documents in this section of the course are all you usually need to close most deals.

PAYOUT AGREEMENT
Send To Buyer

The PAYOUT AGREEMENT is more specific to a particular deal than the NON-CIRCUMVENT AGREEMENT. This will actually state the amount that the note seller and note finder (you) will receive upon the closing of escrow.

(Note Buyer's Name) agrees to pay **(Your Name) ($Your Fee)** and **(Note Seller's Name) ($Buyer's Offer Less Your Fee)** upon closing the note deal for the Property Address: **(Street Address, City, State, and Zip)**. This agreement will be included in the escrow instructions for this transaction.

As stated above, **(Your Name)** will receive **($Your Fee)**, **(Your Fee Written in Words)** dollars upon closing of escrow and payment shall be made to:

(Your Name)
(Your Street Address)
(Your City, State and Zip)

Also stated above, **(Seller's Name)** will receive **($Buyer's Offer Less Your Fee)**, **(Buyer's Offer Less Your Fee Written in Words)** dollars upon closing of escrow and payment shall be made to:

(Seller's Name)
(Seller's Street Address)
(Seller's City, State and Zip)

Signed:

_____   _____   _____
  (Your Signature)   **(Your Printed Name)**   **(Date)**

_____   _____   _____
  (Seller's Signature)   **(Seller's Printed Name)**   **(Date)**

TELEPHONE SCRIPTS / EXAMPLE PHONE CONVERSATIONS

In the next few pages, I will go over a few highly effective scripts and example phone conversations that could be applicable to any situation you encounter. Remember, the scripts are available at **www.notefindersresourcekit.com**. Please read through them and get familiar and comfortable with their content. Also, feel free to mix and match the scripts to create something that feels most comfortable for you.

Script 1: Getting Information On A Note For Sale

The telephone script below is designed to give you an idea of what to say to your prospective note seller. Remember, you want to be comfortable with what you are saying and not come across as though you are reading. Once you have obtained the information required, you can then post that information on the website for an offer from one of the note buyers. The web address is: **www.notenetwork.com/Noteservice**. By submitting notes on the free note service you could earn quick cash profits for each transaction. Better yet, you have the opportunity to connect with qualified, pre-screened note buyers who are looking for notes like the ones you're finding and submitting.

Introduction:

"Hi **(Note Holder's First Name)**, this is **(Your Name)**. I'm interested in the property you sold recently. Are you still receiving monthly payments from that sale?"

IF YES: "I'd like to offer you a free quote to let you know what your payments are worth today (Proceed to question 1)."
IF NO: "What happened? Did they pay it off or was it refinanced?"

*NOTE: When asking the following questions it is best to ask them in an informal manner. Do not make it sound as though you are reading from a script as this will sound unprofessional and unprepared. Also, remember to be friendly while getting the information you need.

1. What kind of interest rate are you getting?_____

2. What is the payment amount?_____

3. How long is the term (original length) of the loan (note)? _____

4. What is the original amount of the loan (note)?_____

5. Is this the 1st or 2nd loan? _____

    5a. (If 2nd ask: What was the amount on the 1st position loan?)

    _____

6. What was the down payment the buyers paid? _____

7. What was the sale price of the property? _____

8. What is the property type (SFR, condo, commercial, or other)? ____

9. What is the property address? _____

10. Are the new buyers living there? _____

11. What was the date of sale? _____

12. What was the date of the first payment? _____

13. Are the payments on time? _____

14. What day of the month are the payments due? _____

15. Is there a balloon payment? _____

    (If so, how much and when is it due?) _____

16. What is the payor's credit score? _____

    16a. (If unknown ask: What does the payor do for a living?)

    _____

17. Have you received any other offers? _____

18. Is there anything else I should know about this note? _____

    _____

"Okay, let me put this information in front of the buyers I work with and I'll call you back as soon as I have an offer for you, okay? Great, I should have something for you soon."

Now post this information on the website at **www.notenetwork.com/Noteservice**. By submitting this information, you could get an idea of what the note is worth to a note buyer.

Once you know what a buyer will pay for the note, simply deduct 4%-8% from that price and offer the remaining amount to the seller. The amount you deduct will be the amount you earn for your efforts. I like to suggest that you try to earn at least $2,000 to $5,000 per deal. On average our students earn $3,600 per deal. Be sure to ask the buyer if they are paying closing costs. Some buyers will not pay closing costs, and you will have to subtract an additional 3% from their offer price to cover these costs.

So, let me give you a quick example of your profits. A note seller has a note to sell. The face value of that note is $33,000. The remaining balance of the note is $30,000 and a buyer will pay $22,000 for it, and they will pay closing. You deduct $2,000 from what the buyer will pay for your fee and offer the seller $20,000 – If the seller says "yes" you just earned a quick cash profit of $2,000.

Script 2: What To Say When You Call Back The Note Seller

"Hi, **(Note Seller's First Name)**, this is **(Your Name)**. I have a purchase price for your note. Do you have a piece of paper and a pencil handy? You will want to write this down."

"Have you ever sold a note before? Let me just briefly explain to you how this process works and how the cash value of your note is determined."

"Each monthly payment you receive is analyzed and its value in the future calculated. In other words, these dollars today will buy more than the same dollars in the future. Let me give you a couple of examples of what I'm talking about."

"Looking back 20 years ago, we could go to the movies for what? About $3.00, right. And gasoline was about $.95 a gallon? Now look at what we pay. This is what I mean when I say dollars today have a greater purchasing power than dollars in the future. So we have to take that into consideration when determining the price for your note."

"Also, suppose I have $100 in my left hand and $50 in my right. Which bill would you like? The $100, right? But now, let's add this to the equation: you have to wait (the remaining years of monthly payments on their note, let's say 8) 8 years to get the $100 or you can have the $50 right now, which one would you rather have? Of course the $50 now, right?"

"Now that you have a better understanding of the process, let's talk about the offer. I have found a buyer willing to offer you **($ Offer From The Buyer Less Your Fees)** for your monthly payments stretching into the future. This amount is a net amount to you and there are no additional fees of any kind. You will get your cash in about 4 weeks. How does that sound?"

If The Seller Says, "I Need To Think About It."

If they say, "I need to think about it," you can say: "Okay, I can appreciate that **(Note Seller's First Name)**, let me also explain how you are guaranteed to get paid."

"When and if you decide to go ahead with this sale, I will send you a COMMITMENT LETTER that states my obligation to you, along with a list of documents I will need from you."

"The buyer will deposit a check in the amount of **($ Offer From the Buyer Less Your Fees)** into an escrow account at a title or escrow company. This company, which we can use in your area if you prefer will make sure you get the right amount of money and that the buyer gets the right paperwork. This way you are guaranteed to get paid."

"So you are guaranteed to receive your money without hassle or risk. Sounds pretty good, doesn't it? This is the same way the deal was closed when you originally sold your property."

"Would you like me to send you this information package today?"

- If yes: Ask for their fax number or confirm their address in order to send the offer in writing. Use the COVER LETTER TO THE COMMITMENT LETTER (page 151) and the COMMITMENT LETTER (pages 148-150) to display the offer. Follow up to ensure they received it and to answer any questions they may have. Continue to follow up every 3 months.

- If no: "Okay, I will follow up with you in the future to see if circumstances have changed. In the meantime, let me give you my name and phone number in the event you change your mind or have questions. What time of the day is best to reach you?" (Continue to follow up every 3 months.)

When The Seller Says, "Yes."

Ask for their fax number or confirm their address and send the COVER LETTER TO THE COMMITMENT LETTER, COMMITMENT LETTER, and INFORMATION REQUEST FORM. Follow up to ensure they have received the documents and answer any questions they may have. Remember, all of these documents are available as part of the Note Finders Resource Kit at: **www.notefindersresourcekit.com**

Script 3: Handling Calls On Postcards
You Sent To Note Owners

This is the script you will use to handle callbacks from note holders to whom you have sent postcards.

You: "Hi **(Note Holders's First Name)**, this is **(Your Name)** returning your call. I'm the one who sent you the postcard in the mail. Are you still collecting payments on the property you sold."

Note Holder: "Yes I am. How did you know about my note?"

You: "Actually, this is public information and it is recorded at the county courthouse. This is where I came upon your information."

Note Holder: "Why are you interested in my note?"

You: "I work with a group of buyers who are interested in purchasing payments secured by real estate. Just like the ones you are collecting! Now, did you originally plan to carry the financing when you sold the house or did you just do it to get the property sold?"

Note Holder: "I guess you could say we did it to get the property sold."

You: "Are the people who bought your property making the payments every month?"

Note Holder: "Yes, but I didn't realize how long a twenty year term actually was!"

You: "I understand and believe I can help you out here. As I said earlier, I work with a group of buyers and would like to make you a cash offer for those future payments. In order to do so I need to gather some information."

Note Holder: "Well, I don't have a copy of the contract in front of me, but I should be able to remember most of the information. What do you need?"

You: (Proceed to the questions portion of Script 1 and gather the note information.)

   *****NOTE**: This script is not absolute. Your experience and conversation may vary. Use this script to give you a general overview on how to handle these conversations and the things you need to say to start earning money and finder's fees quickly.

Script 4: Questions To Ask On Various Property Types

For various property types, you also want to find out a few extra things when collecting information on the note. Here are some additional pieces of information that buyers may ask you for.

Mobile Home Note:

- What are the year, the make, and the model of the mobile home?

- What is the condition of the mobile home?

- Does the mobile home include land?

- Is the mobile home on owned land or in a park?

    - (If on land) What is the size of the lot?

    - (If in a park) Ask the following:

        - What is the park quality?

        - What is the rent for the space?

        - How many spaces are in the park?

        - What park amenities are available?

Land Note:

- How is the land zoned?

- How large is the plot of land (acres)?

- Where is the land located? Is it a prime buildable lot, vacation resort lot, metro lot, or rural lot?

- How is the land used? Is the land raw acreage, agricultural, timberland, or something else?

- What improvements are there? Is it semi-improved or improved land?

- Are the access roads maintained? (if it's rural)

Commercial Property Note:

- How is the property being used?

- What is the operating history of the land (not the business)?

Script 5: Establishing Contact With Real Estate Agents

The following script will help you when contacting Real Estate Agents.

You: "Hello **(Real Estate Agent's First Name)**, this is **(Your Name)**. I am a cashflow specialist and I believe I can be of help to you and your clients. May I ask you a few questions?"

Agent: "Sure."

You: "Do you sell properties where the seller carries back some or all of the financing?"

Agent: "Yes."

You: "Great! Do you ever have clients who would have preferred their cash up front instead of over time?"

Agent: "Yes, all the time!"

You: "I can help in these situations. What I do is help get people cash now for future payments. If you run into anyone who would prefer a lump sum of cash please pass my contact information along. Again, my name is

(Your Name) and I can be reached at **(Your Telephone Number)** or by email at **(Your Email Address)**."

Agent: "I will be sure to do so and thanks for calling."

You: "You are very welcome and I look forward to being of service to you and your clients."

*NOTE: This script is not absolute. Your experience and conversation may vary. Use this script to give you a general overview on how to handle these conversations and the things you need to say to begin building a professional relationship with a Real Estate Agent.

Script 6: Establishing Contact With Escrow/Title Agents

This is a script that will provide you with direction when contacting Escrow/Title Agents.

You: "Hello **(Escrow/Title Agent's First Name)**, this is **(Your Name)**. I'm calling because I may be able to be of help to you. Now, is most of your business from real estate sales?"

Escrow/Title Agent: "Yes."

You: "Great! Do you ever come across real estate sales where the seller has carried all or a portion of the financing?"

Escrow/Title Agent: "We sure do!"

You: "Well, what I do is help people get cash now for future payments. Would you mind passing my contact information along to interested parties?"

Escrow/Title Agent: "Sure."

You: "Perfect! My name is **(Your Name)** and I can be reached at **(Your Telephone Number)** or by email at **(Your Email Address)**."

You: "Also, many of the buyers I work with need closing services for their deals. I will be sure to send them your way."

Escrow/Title Agent: "Thank you."

You: "You are welcome and I look forward to working with you in the future."

*NOTE: This script is not absolute. Your experience and conversation may vary. Use this script to give you a general overview on how to handle these conversations and the things you need to say to begin building a professional relationship with an Escrow/Title Agent.

Script 7: Establishing Contact With Builders Who May Have Notes To Sell

As I mentioned earlier builders can be great sources of notes. The following script will help you get an understanding of how to approach them.

You: "Hello, is **(Builder's First Name)** in?"

You: "Hi **(Builder's First Name)**, my name is **(Your Name)**. I've been able to help other builders like you get their hands on their cash when they need it – without borrowing. I'd like to show you how I might be of help to you as well."

You: "Now, when you finish a project, sometimes you carry part of the financing when you sell it. That paper is nice to hold for the monthly income, but sometimes you could accomplish more if you had a large chunk of cash right now. Do you know what I mean?"

Builder: "Sure. I am always looking for ways to free up cash that I have tied up."

You: "Great. I can be of help to you. See, I work with a group of buyers interested in payments secured by property such as the projects you are completing."

You: "Do you have any notes that you'd like to hear a cash offer on?"

Builder: "I've got a couple."

You: "Perfect! I just need some information." (Proceed to questions portion of Script 1.)

Script 8: Following Up With Professionals Once You've Mailed Them

I encourage you to make follow up phone calls to the professionals you sent postcards, brochures or newsletters. Just a quick, simple phone call to them, will do. This can be fun and exciting because you will be developing a business relationship with them. You will not be selling them anything, which they will greatly appreciate. This will help them to remember you and hopefully they will refer any notes that come across their desk in the future.

Your follow-up call can be as simple as:

"Hi this is **(Your Name)** and I'm just following up to see if you received my recent newsletter, "Creative Financing Journal," and to see if you have any questions that I might be able to answer (If so, address their questions)."

(After you have addressed any questions) "Do you have any clients I can help at this time?" (If yes, and they have the information at hand, proceed to the questions portion of Script 1. If yes, but the information is not at hand, then determine a time to call back.)

(If the professional does not have any clients you can help at this time.) "Well, feel free to give me a call if any questions come up as I'd love to be of service to you and your clients. I'll also follow up next quarter to see if any questions may have come up."

Isn't that simple?

This closing will let them know that you're interested in establishing a relationship with them; this may spark their interest and create a desire to keep their eyes and ears open for opportunities to benefit the both of you.

It's very important to understand that as you do this, you are filling your pipeline and you could have professionals calling you with their clients' notes! You could be setting yourself up for business and all you'll need to do is be available to answer your phone calls. This is the real key to building your business.

This is your chance to author your own life! It makes me very happy to support you all the way through this process – to watch you achieve your goals of being your own boss, being able to pay your bills and have time to yourself.

You may be able to take those vacations whenever you want and still set yourself up for a comfortable retirement. This is what brings me satisfaction. My staff and I will be here to support you all the way! Feel free to email us at **support@dalbeyeducation.com** and we will be happy to help.

Determining the Value of Real Estate IOUs

SELECTING THE BEST REAL ESTATE NOTES

Here are some ideas on how to select the very best real estate notes to work with. I am going to teach you how to determine whether a note is secured or not. If it's a well secured note and you are helping someone sell it, then you could of course, sell it for more money and make a larger referral fee.

Perhaps you have heard about mortgage companies or institutional lenders selling trust deeds or mortgages that are guaranteed. Have you ever heard of a guaranteed note? I want to say those guarantees are about as good as the company that backs it. Too many of these companies have now gone out of business.

The guarantee I am going to show you is one that you'll want to consider. It's a guarantee that you are going to get paid for the deals that close.

Number one, when analyzing a note, buyers will look at the security of the note. I will always consider the property value first. We can determine the value of a property from a recent sales price for which the property sold for or by a current appraisal from a licensed appraiser. <u>Personally, for me the best indicator of the value of the property is the price it sold for</u>. It could appraise at $130,000 but it sold at $100,000. What price are most note buyers going to use? The price it sold for, $100,000. The selling price is always the real value of the property.

Starting with the property value ($100,000), I then look at the loans on record for the property. Let's say there is a $50,000 first position loan and a $30,000 second position loan. So I have $80,000 worth of loans on this property and now I want to determine what the equity is. The property value, minus the total amount of loans, equals the equity. Take $100,000 minus $80,000 worth of loans and get $20,000 (20%) equity in the property.

Let's talk about a factor called the Combined Loan to Value, or CLTV. The Combined Loan to Value ratio is simply your lien plus any senior liens on the property, divided by the total property value. Here I would add the $30,000 second position loan to the $50,000 first position loan to get $80,000 and divide it by the property value of $100,000. This will give me .80 or 80% CLTV.

The protective equity on a property, or gross equity cushion, and the Combined Loan to Value ratio are what I look at to see how secure a particular loan or note is. Protective equity is equal to the property value minus the total loans on the property.

What about the protective equity, or a gross equity cushion, for both loans on this property? Obviously each of these loans has a different range of security doesn't it?

If I was the owner of the first loan of $50,000 and the property is worth $100,000, how much equity cushion or protective equity would I have for that loan? The answer is $50,000. I would take $100,000 minus the $50,000 of my loan and that leaves $50,000. Now let's take a look at the Loan to Value ratio for the first position loan. $50,000 loan divided by $100,000 value gives me a 50% LTV.

Now on the second loan, which is $30,000, I have the same $100,000 property however, this time $100,000 minus $80,000 of total loans (my loan and the senior loan) leaves $20,000 protected equity.

When I take the $80,000 in total loans and (that's my loan plus the senior) divide by $100,000 property value, I see the CLTV went up to 80%. So the second loan isn't quite as secure as the first loan.

Many banks and other institutional lenders consider 80% loan to value ratio about as high as they want to go. Any percentage higher than that may be considered too risky. Note buyers decide in their dealings what kind of Combined Loan to Value (CLTV) ratio they are happy with and what kind of protective equity they want. Most buyers prefer to see 80% CLTV or lower. But here's another consideration – something called Combined Investment to Value.

Combined Investment to Value or CITV is simply any senior loans on the property plus my offer on the note divided by the value of the property. So, let's take the above example of a $100,000 property. I have a $50,000 1st loan and a $30,000 2nd, which for this example is the note I am buying. Let's say I purchased the 2nd for $25,000. My Combined Investment to Value is 75%. I have the $50,000 1st, and my investment on the 2nd of $25,000 which totals $75,000.

Divide $75,000 into $100,000 and I get a Combined Investment to Value ratio of 75%. Even though I have a high CLTV ratio, I can still reduce my risk when I look at my Combined Investment to Value ratio. The higher the CLTV or CITV, the more risk they take on because the buyer will take less protective equity. The lower the CLTV ratio, the better for the buyer and the more money you could make when referring the note.

Now in our example, with all things being equal, both of these loans are probably pretty well secured. The 1st position loan is most secure and the 2nd position loan is a little less secure. Note buyers determine their risk factors and make purchases based on those factors.

Remember, both of these liens can go to foreclosure. The first to complete the foreclosure process is in the driver's seat. They will have the edge in terms of controlling the foreclosure.

What kind of document is recorded to protect the note holder's interest in the note? The answer – a "Request for Notice of Default." The buyer can get the sample forms for the "Request for Notice of Default" from the title insurance company, their attorney or stationery store. Recording is proof that you requested notice. A smart note buyer will communicate directly with other lien holders to make sure that, in the event of default, they will be informed of this status.

Also, many people are confused about whether a holder of a second note can foreclose if they don't get their payments. Most have heard, "If the holder of the first files foreclosure, they get paid off in full and all the rest of the loans are wiped out." A second or even third position note holder can foreclose, but now must keep the payments current on all loans in front of them.

You see, a note holder can foreclose whether they have a first, second, third or even maybe a seventh lien on the property. A note holder has the right to foreclosure to protect their interest. It gets a little more complicated the further down the chain the note holder happens to be, but they definitely have the right to foreclose.

What about the due on sale clauses on the senior liens? Let's say that I hold a second and the first loan has a due on sale clause and then I end up foreclosing. First of all, if the first loan were an FHA loan, VA loan, or a private party loan, there is a chance that it might not have a due on sale clause, so that's the very first thing that I would check. That's one way that it could go, so there wouldn't be any problem in taking over the property in that case when I foreclose on my second position note.

Otherwise, let's say that the first is a corporate lender and is somebody who can enforce a "due on sale clause," I would begin to think that I might have a problem there if I get the property back at the sale by foreclosing on my second position note. I would feel that they might say, "Well, this was a sale of the property, and you are going to have to renegotiate the loan with them." Well, I probably won't have to, because foreclosing on a property is generally alright in terms of getting around the "due on sale clause." This is a good way to get a property without having to qualify for it.

REVIEW OF KEY POINTS

Remember, equity is the main factor in determining the security of a note. A note buyer can measure their protective equity by the Combined Loan to Value ratio, which is their gross equity cushion. This is how much equity there is beyond the loan when it's added to any senior loan. If I am trying to find the protective equity on my note where there is a first and a second and I have the second, I would add the first and second loan together and then subtract that total from the value of the property. This number is your protective equity or gross equity cushion.

Another thing to keep in mind is that senior liens are generally more secure than junior liens. A senior lien holder always has the same amount of protective equity regardless of how many junior liens are stacked below it.

This is something people often ask about – if they own a property and it has a $50,000 loan – can they put a $30,000 second on it without asking the holder of the first? What do you think? Do you need to ask them for permission? No! And the reason you don't have to ask is because, you could put a second, third, fourth, fifth, anything behind that loan and the first lien holder would still have the same exact protective equity and same Combined Loan to Value ratio.

If I was a junior lien holder, I would file a notice of default or have my escrow company do it for me after I purchased the note. I would also send a letter to the senior lender telling them that I'd be happy to make up any late payments if they will inform me. Remember, any lien holder can foreclose.

Most people don't know this information that you are learning. I am so excited for you because I know this information can change your life – just like it has done for me.

NOTE GRADING AND PRICING GUIDELINES

One of the greatest advantages you can give yourself as a note finder is knowing how to price a seller financed real estate note. Although this skill is not necessary to be successful as a note finder, it is important for anyone looking to make the most money possible from every note deal.

There are six main areas that I look at when pricing a real estate note. Each of these criteria has a different level of importance:

1. Equity in the property (50% of the evaluation)

2. Credit score of the payor (20% of the evaluation)

3. Payment history or late payments (20% of the evaluation)

4. The number of payments that have been made or "seasoning" (10% of the evaluation)

5. The type of real estate note

6. The position of the note

Using these guidelines, you can easily figure out what most note buyers will pay for the note you've found. Once you know what a note buyer will pay, you can simply deduct a fair fee from that price, which could be $500, $2,000, $5,000 or much much more depending on the size of the note and what the seller needs. Remember, as a general rule, I suggest 4%-8% as a basis for your finder's fee.

What is left will be approximately what the note seller could expect to receive for their note, less closing costs.

For example, let's say Sam Seller's note balance is $25,000. After using the Note Grading and Pricing Guidelines (NGPG) to evaluate it, you may find that the note is worth $21,500 to a buyer. As the note finder, you could deduct $2,000 for your finder's fee. Keep in mind the fee of $2,000 is not a "standard fee." Fees vary depending on several factors, including the size of the note, the buyer's bid and the seller's needs or requirements. $21,500 minus $2,000 equals $19,500 for Sam Seller, but remember – there are closing costs too.

To be safe, I usually deduct $1,000 or 3% (whichever is higher) for closing costs. This will help to ensure that there is enough money to cover closing without having to dip into my calculated finder's fee. Remember, whatever is not used in closing typically goes to you – the note finder.

So, in this example, after deducting a referral fee of $2,000 and closing costs of $1,000 (3% is only $645), you would be left with $18,500 to Sam Seller.

In the example above, Sam Seller would receive $18,500 in cash now for his note. So by applying the Note Grading and Pricing Guidelines, I can have a good idea of what the seller could expect to receive from a buyer – even before finding someone to buy it.

Now that you understand how having this knowledge works to your advantage, let's take a look at Note Grading and Pricing Guidelines in more detail. The first four criteria – Equity, Credit score, Payment History, Number of Payments Made (Seasoning) have a score chart associated with them. Using specific guidelines and the scoring charts, we give each of the first four factors a score. We then simply add the scores together to arrive at a total score for the note. Then we use the last two charts, which take the property type and note position into account, to arrive at a safe Yield for buyers to aim for when purchasing a note. This Yield percentage will allow you to easily calculate what a note buyer would likely offer for that particular note.

It's six simple steps, and it requires virtually no math.

I'll walk you through an example step-by-step.

As mentioned, one of the most important areas is evaluating the amount of equity in the property. Equity is simply the difference between the market value of the property and what the payor still owes on their property. This parameter can make or break the deal and is considered to be the "trump card" for any note deal. As a result, the score for equity makes up a full 50% of the total score for the note itself. To come up with a score for the equity portion of the Note Grading and Pricing Guidelines, we calculate the amount of equity in the property and plug it into the next chart.

For our example, let's say I have a house that sold for $100,000 – that is its market value. There is just one loan on the property. It's a seller financed loan in the amount of $70,000. How much equity is in the property? That's right, it's $30,000, or 30% of the sales price.

$100,000 (Market Value) - $70,000 (Loan Amount) = $30,000

And $30,000 ÷ $100,000 = 30%

	EQUITY				SCORE
1.	50.1%	To	100%	=	50
	30.1%	To	50.0%	=	45
	20.1%	To	30.0%	=	40
	12.1%	To	20.0%	=	35
	5.1%	To	12.0%	=	30
	0%	To	5.0%	=	25
	EQUITY SCORE			=	40

Now before we calculate how many points we will give for the equity portion, let's look over a few items in the equity chart. First, notice that the figures on the left side represent the percentage of equity in the property. Next, you will see that as the amount of equity in a property goes up, our score for the equity portion goes up as well. So the more points we give here, the better.

Also, there is an upper and lower end to each range in the equity chart. The lower end of the range in each line for each point total represents the least amount of equity required to give the corresponding score, while the "upper" end of the range is the most amount of equity required for that score. So in this example, we determined that the property securing Sam Seller's note has 30% equity in it. What score would we give that? That's right, we would write in 40 points in the following chart for step 1.

Now that we have calculated our Equity score, we move on to the Credit portion. For many note buyers, the credit of the payor (i.e., the person making payments on the note) is very important. That's why the Credit score is second in importance only to Equity in the Note Grading and Pricing Guidelines.

Credit makes up 20% of the total score. Just as we did when we calculated the Equity score, we will take information given to us by the note holder and plug it into a specific chart for this area.

The Credit scores that we see generally range from the mid 400's to well above 700. This figure gives us an idea of how the payor has been doing with their debts, including credit cards. Higher Credit scores tell us that the payor has good credit. And the better the credit the more valuable the note.

Here are general guidelines that will help you understand Credit scores and what they mean:

1. Above 700 – Payor's score is excellent, considered to be A+ credit
2. 651 to 700 – Payor's score is very good, considered to be A credit
3. 601 to 650 – Payor's score is good, considered to be B credit
4. 551 to 600 – Payor's score is average, considered to be C credit
5. 501 to 550 – Payor's score is below average, considered to be D credit
6. 000 to 500 – Payor has poor credit
7. No Credit – Payor has no credit payment history

Before we calculate how many points we will give for the Credit portion, let's examine the Credit chart to understand it. The figures in the chart represent different ranges of Credit scores. The higher the Credit score, the more points we will give.

There is also an upper and lower end to each range in the Credit chart. The lower end of the range for each point total sets the lowest Credit score required to give the corresponding score, while the upper end of the range represents the highest Credit rating required for that score.

So let's say that the payor on Sam Seller's note has a Credit score of 650. We take this information and plug it into the next chart to arrive at our score for the Credit portion. As you can see, a Credit score of 650 correlates to 16 points here in step 2. That's what we write in the chart.

2.

CREDIT SCORE				SCORE
701	To	900	=	20
651	To	700	=	18
601	To	650	=	16
551	To	600	=	14
No History	To	No History	=	12
501	To	550	=	10
0	To	500	=	8
CREDIT SCORE	=	650	=	**16**

Next, we must take delinquent payments into consideration with the Payment History. This is another very important factor, and it makes up another 20% of the total score. The information needed to arrive at the Payment History score comes from Sam Seller's loan payment record. If all payments have been made on time, we consider the payments to be current. So for this example, let's assume that Sam Seller's note is current. If 12 payments have been made, we would write in 16 points for the Payment score in the chart for step 3.

3.

PAYMENT HISTORY	SCORE
Current, more than 30 payments have been made	20
Current, 13 to 30 payments have been made	18
Current, **7 to 12** payments made have been made	16
Current, less than 6 payments have been made	14
Payments more than 30 days late within last 2 years	0
PAYMENT HISTORY SCORE =	**16**

Finally, we look at the number of payments made, also referred to as Seasoning. This score is directly related to the number of payments made without taking late payments into consideration. To calculate the Seasoning score, we count up the number of payments made and plug that into the Seasoning chart. As with the Equity and Credit scores, the same rules apply to the upper and lower ends for each line in the chart. So if Sam Seller sold his property 12 months ago and all of the payments on the note were made, then we would give four points for the Seasoning score in the chart for step 4.

4.

MONTHS OF SEASONING				SCORE
37	or	More	=	10
25	to	36	=	8
13	to	24	=	6
7	to	12	=	4
4	to	6	=	2
0	to	3	=	0
	SEASONING SCORE		=	**4**

To get the Total Score for Sam Seller's note, just add the four scores together from the previous four charts. Here's the simple addition:

Equity Score	=	40 +
Credit Score	=	16 +
Payment Score	=	16 +
Seasoning Score	=	4
TOTAL SCORE	=	**76**

Now, apply the Total Score of 76 to this grading chart:

SCORE				GRADE
85	to	100	=	AAA
75	to	84	=	AA
65	to	74	=	A
55	to	64	=	AB
45	to	54	=	B
35	to	44	=	C
0	to	34	=	D

So you can see that because Sam Seller's note has a Total Score of 76, it's rated an AA note as per our grading thus far. Next, we will look at the Type of Note chart (step 5) to see how we will rate Sam Seller's note.

As we know, many different types of property can secure a note. The property securing the note is what the note buyer gets if they have to foreclose. Because the real estate is what protects the note buyer's investment, it is important to include this factor into our pricing procedures.

Property types range from condominiums (condos) and mobile homes (MH) to single-family residences (SFRs), and they can be occupied by the payors themselves (owner occupied) or rented out (non owner occupied). Each of these property types is priced differently.

We can account for these various property types by placing them into one of four categories. Category 1 notes are considered to be the most valuable or safe, while category 4 notes tend to see the lowest offers because the properties securing them are not as desirable.

To illustrate this, let's assume that Sam Seller's note is secured by a house that is considered to be a single-family residence, and the payor lives in it. What category would we put this in?

Category 1 is exactly right: Owner Occupied Single Family Residence.

5.

TYPE OF NOTE

1	2	3	4
Owner Occupied Single Family Residence	Owner Occupied Condos & Multi-units	Owner Occupied Mobile Homes that include land, Non Owner Occupied Single Family Residences	Non Owner Occupied Mobile Homes, Condos & Multi Units **All 2nd Liens (2)**

Now we move to the last chart – step 6 – to calculate the Maximum Investment to Value (MaxITV) and Yield a note buyer will use to make an offer. Step 6 is actually a two-part process – MaxITV and Yield. The numbers 1 – 4 at the top of the chart correspond to the category number of the note, while the numbers in parenthesis tell us when to apply the footnotes below. You will calculate both the MaxITV and Yield figures separately, and then use the lower of the two numbers as your offer.

The MaxITV is the most a buyer can safely pay for the note based on the property value. On our Sam Seller example note, we determined in step 4 and step 5 that it is Category 1 AA. You can see in the next chart that the MaxITV for a 1 AA note is 75%. So, multiply the property value (it was $100,000, remember?) by 75%, and the MaxITV figure is $75,000.

Now, let's take a look at the Yield percentage section of the next chart. Typically buyers will calculate to the high side of each Yield range, so it is safest for us to use the highest Yield possible when calculating a price for Sam's note. (A higher Yield or return means the note buyer will pay less for the note.)

Because Sam Seller's note was graded AA, consulting the step 6 chart shows that the desired Yield would fall between 12.5% and 15.5%. If we calculate to the high side, our Yield will be 15.5%.

The low end of each range is typically reserved for negotiating purposes. In other words, if Sam Seller rejects the offer calculated using a Yield of 15.5%, we know we can still lower our yield in order to arrive at a higher price.

So for Sam Seller's note, the lowest Yield we should see is 12.5%, but we will start with a Yield of 15.5%. Remember, the lower the Yield, the more we can offer on the note. The higher the Yield, the less it's worth. So the Yield is typically what the note buyer will think about when pricing the note.

In order to calculate an actual price based on that 15.5% Yield, you need to use a financial calculator and know the details of the note – the number of payments, interest rate, and payment amount.

6.

YIELD OR PRICE

Note Grade	1	2	3	4	Wholesale Yields
AAA	80% (1)	75% (1)	70% (1)	65% (1)	12.0% - 15.0%
AA	75% (1)	70% (1)	65% (1)	60% (1)	12.5% - 15.5%
A	70%	65%	60% (1)	57% (1)	13.0% - 16.0%
AB	65%	60%	57%	55%	14.0% - 17.0%
B	60%	55%	50%	50%	15.0% - 18.0%
C	55%	55%	50%	50%	17.0% - 20.0%
D	50%	50%	45%	45%	19.0% - 22.0%

Finally, there are occasions when we must adjust our MaxITV and Yields. This is especially true when one of the two footnotes apply. Remember, we only make these adjustments when we come across a note category or MaxITV with a footnote number next to it.

Here's what each footnote means and when we apply them.

Footnote 1 – Reduce MaxITV by 10% if equity is less than 10%. For example, if we are looking at a Category 1 AAA note, but there is less than 10% equity, our MaxITV should be reduced to 70%.

Footnote 2 – Reduce MaxITV by 10% and increase Wholesale Yield by 5% when working with 2nd position notes. For example, if we were dealing with an AAA second position note, our MaxITV would be reduced to 55% and our Wholesale Yield should be increased to 20%.

Remember, first position notes are more secure than second position notes – that's why all second position notes are scored category 4 for Type of Note. As a result, second position notes will see a deeper discount.

Now that you understand the Note Grading and Pricing Guidelines and the charts above, you can begin to use them to make more on each deal.

As I said at the beginning of this section, mastering the Note Grading and Pricing Guidelines is not required to be successful, but it will help you when working with "Sam Seller" or anyone else you know that is looking to sell their note. With this additional knowledge, you will be ready to make the most money from each note deal that you do.

CHAPTER 9

The Ten Biggest Mistakes Note Holders Make That Could Affect Your Deals

A REAL ESTATE SECRET SUCCESS STORY

"Every day in this country seller financed notes are created... this is very simple just follow the course and you will make money. I've made $179,947.19 so far."

- Student, Dan B., New York

I've talked a lot so far about how working real estate deals with notes can make you tens of thousands of dollars, but there are plenty of mistakes that many note buyers and sellers make that could cost you money as well.

In this chapter, I will alert you to the common errors that people make when constructing these deals. Any one of these mistakes could cost you money and could cost you a deal… but if you read and remember these solutions, you won't fall into these potential traps and you could potentially get more deals done.

You can use this information to help you better educate your note sellers and thus turn more prospects into customers.

1. **Not recording the contract at the county recorder's office:**

   When a note holder doesn't record the contract, a lien is not placed on the property. If legal action were filed for one reason or another, the note holder's attorney or the judge may say that the document is not legal or enforceable. This means that the note holder can not legally foreclose on the property if the payor doesn't make their payments.

   This could be a problem for note finders trying to help get the note sold. If the note is not legally secured by property, many buyers will avoid it… making it difficult to sell.

   Rule #1: Make sure the contract is recorded!

2. **Not enforcing the contract or forgiving late payments:**

   Does the contract have a penalty clause for late payments? If so, that penalty clause needs to be enforced. This is extra money in the note holder's pocket. Enforcing the penalty clause also sends the message to the payor that the note holder means business.

   If the payment is not received within the grace period, the note holder can send a certified letter (return receipt requested) to enforce the contract. This letter should notify the buyer that if this contract is not current within XXX days, then legal action –

possibly foreclosure, or whatever action necessary as stated under the default section of the contract – will result.

If this doesn't produce results, the note holder should then turn it over to an attorney experienced in foreclosures and real estate law in that state.

This situation presents problems for note finders because it is at times difficult to sell delinquent notes. There are, of course, buyers that specialize in delinquent notes but even delinquent note buyers have issues dealing with notes that were not enforced properly.

Rule #2: Make sure the note holder starts enforcing the contract!

3. **Not maintaining thorough records:**

    Note holders should keep close track of the day they receive their monthly or scheduled payment. A good practice is to always photocopy the check and the bank deposit receipt, or to keep a separate bank account exclusively for accepting the note payments. This practice provides recorded proof that the payments have been paid, and WHEN they were paid.

    If there is a dispute with the payor, or if the note holder decides to sell the note to a note buyer, that buyer will need to see proof of payment. (Also, the note holder should always deposit funds received as soon as possible after they receive them).

    If the payments are collected by a bank or escrow company, the information needed may be requested, and these institutions will furnish the note holder with a payment ledger and account balance.

    As a note finder, you should always try to collect as much accurate and detailed information as possible. This will help to make your deals run smoothly and will help them to close in a timely manner. Remember, a note buyer will need to know all of the details about the payment stream they are buying. If they are missing some information or some supporting documents, it will be difficult for a buyer to know what is actually for sale and it could possibly prevent the deal from ever going through.

Rule #3: Always try to find an accurate recording of the payment stream!

4. **Not keeping documents safe:**

Can the note holder locate all the documents? Remember: the documents may be needed at any time – if the note holder wants to sell the note for cash, if the payor pays off the note early, or if the property that is securing the note is sold or transferred to a new owner.

The note holder should put the documents in a safe place away from fire or theft, as they may be needed tomorrow, a year from now, or even 25 years in the future. Put it this way – wouldn't you kick yourself if you couldn't immediately locate the paperwork that could make you a lot of money? As a note finder, you'll want to make sure that all of the documents are organized and ready for when the buyer needs them. Be sure to send the seller the information request form and let the seller know that all of the documents will be needed to close the deal.

Rule #4: Make sure the note holder has all of documentation organized and stored in a safe place!

5. **Not keeping taxes up to date:**

There is always the possibility of default with the payor. If the property goes into default and then enters foreclosure, who is responsible for the taxes being paid? The note holder is, as that individual is the lien holder of the real estate note.

A note holder should obtain a copy of the paid tax bill from the payor or check with the county or city assessor's office to make sure the taxes are current. It is possible that the property could be sold for back taxes.

Delinquent taxes could pose a problem when the note is being sold. In the process of closing a note deal, the title company will always check to make sure the taxes are up to date. All back taxes must be settled before the note is sold.

Rule #5: Make sure the taxes are up to date. If they are not up to date, let the seller know that they will have to bring them current before the note can be sold. Correcting this before the going to closing table will help to prevent this from becoming an issue.

6. **Not regularly inspecting the property:**

When was the last time the note holder saw the property? It's a good idea for the note holder to drive by the property from time to time to see if the building and grounds are well maintained. If the yard and exterior of the building are in good condition or show improvements since it was sold, chances are the inside of the house is being looked after as well.

According to most real estate contracts, the payor must protect and keep up the value of the property. This will be the note holder's (lien holder's) security in case the payor doesn't make the payments. If the property looks run down, the note holder can check the contract for a clause that mandates that the payor keep the premises and building in as good or better condition as they were on the date of sale.

The note holder can send a certified letter, return receipt requested, notifying the payor of the default of the contract and follow through with the recommendations as stated in the contract. Taking a no-nonsense approach in protecting the quality of the property can make it surprisingly easy for the note holder to convince the payor to "clean up his act."

Most note buyers are not happy with property that is not maintained properly. Remember, the property is the collateral that secures the debt. So in a foreclosure situation, the note buyer would foreclose on the property in an effort to recoup their investment. But keep in mind they will only get their money back after they sell the property. If the property is not well maintained, the note buyer will have to invest additional money into the property just to bring it to a sellable condition. As you would expect, many note buyers are not in the rehabbing business and would stay away from property that would need a considerable amount of work in a foreclosure situation.

Rule #6: As a note finder, you'll want to make sure the property securing the note is well maintained. If it's not, suggest that the seller encourage the payor to fix up the property so it is in good condition when the note buyer has the property appraised. Note holders should look after the property by making sure the buyer does too!

7. **Not being aware of subordination clauses:**

If the property buyer (the future payor) requests a subordination clause, the note holder should NOT DO IT. The note holder should confirm this with a real estate attorney but a subordination clause typically gives the buyer the ability to put a senior lien or loan on the contract. This will move the note holder's lien to a second position and will damage the cash value of the note if the note holder decides to sell the contract or any partial payments of the contract.

As you gain experience in the note business, you learn that notes in the first position are more valuable and are easier to sell than notes in the second or even third position. This not to say that you should avoid working with junior liens (you should work with every note you come across). But you don't want to present a first position note to a buyer and have it turn out that there is another senior loan on the property.

Rule #7: A buyer will always have a title search completed before purchasing a note. This will ensure that the note is in the position the buyer was expecting. But the closing table is not the time for surprises. As a finder, you'll want to make sure the seller knows what position their note is in and you'll want to ask if there are any subordination clauses that could change things.

8. **Not keeping insurance up to date:**

    Delinquent hazard insurance could present an issue at the closing table as well. If the hazard insurance policy has not been paid, then the property doesn't have coverage in the event of a fire or other natural disaster, which could mean a total loss for the note holder if such an event were to occur.

    A note holder can call the insurance company to see that hazard insurance is still enforced. They can also have themselves named as a beneficiary as a lien holder for the full amount of the contract. This ensures that any copies of renewal notices are sent to both parties of the real estate contract.

    Most note buyers will want to make sure the hazard insurance is current before they move forward with the purchase of a note. If the insurance is not up to date, the payor or note holder will either have to make insurance payments to bring the policy current or apply for a new hazard insurance all together. Either way, a lapsed hazard insurance policy could slow down or prevent a deal from going through.

    Rule #8: Make sure the hazard insurance is current!

9. **Not reporting note payments as taxable income:**

    The interest information is important for two reasons:

    1) The Note Holder must declare earned interest on their income taxes.

2) The Note Holder needs to provide the total interest figure to the property buyer, so they can file it with their income taxes. Failure to do either of these things could have financial repercussions... and nobody likes a run-in with the IRS.

Rule #9: Make sure the seller is keeping their note deal finances in order. The same goes for you as well. Most buyers will need you to fill out the necessary tax documents before they pay your finder's fee.

10. **Not understanding the value of the contract:**

Note holders should have a good understanding of the factors that affect their note's value, how much their contract is worth in cash, and how quickly they could obtain the funds. As a note finder, you don't waste a motivated and serious note buyer's time by offering to sell a real estate note, and then demanding an unreasonable sales price for the remaining payments.

Rule #10: As a note finder, you should always let the seller know that they will likely receive a discounted offer.

Some of these points may seem a bit obvious, but you would be simply astonished to find out what a large percentage of individuals who hold notes make many of these errors.

Just a little knowledge and effort goes a LONG way in protecting – or increasing – the value of a secured note and your finders fee. If you're a note finder who works with individuals or small businesses that hold notes, using this information to make sure that they are acting responsibly to protect their interests can quickly bring them to trust you and respect your knowledge.

That means they'll probably turn to you immediately if and when they decide it's time to sell their real estate note... which could lead to big profits for you down the line.

Conclusion

Dear Friend,

We've covered a lot of ground here... you now have a lot of valuable information that isn't available anywhere else. In fact, there are a lot of real estate professionals and property investors who aren't familiar with everything that I've taught you in this book.

Even if some of the things you've just learned are not immediately applicable, I can practically guarantee: someday, you'll be able to benefit from the ideas and guidelines in this book, so hold on to it, and be ready to refer to it in the future. These principles could literally MAKE you tens of thousands of dollars.

I've shown you how understanding the seller financed real estate note business and working as a note finder could make you a substantial finder's fee on every deal.

I've shared with you the simple steps you could take to become a successful note finder. I have given examples of the proven methods many of my students have used on their way to success.

And of course, I walked you through an entire deal from start to finish so you know exactly what to expect when you work on your first deal.

I realize that just reading this book may not make you feel like an expert note finder. But I assure you that you now know more than most people getting started in the seller financed note business. So have confidence in yourself and get started building your note finding business by simply talking to people about selling their monthly payments for a lump sum of cash now. Then simply gather the information about their note and let us know if you need help.

Remember, knowledge that isn't used, is lost – so it is imperative that you take what you have learned from this book and begin to apply it by simply talking to others.

Can you picture yourself in Hawaii telling the world about your successes? Once you have made money using the information in this book, please let us know about it. Tell us about your experience and you may very well be telling the world about your success on our next television show! To tell us your story, go to:

http://notenetwork.com/yoursuccess.

I want to congratulate you on your decision to learn more about the best business in the world – the Seller Financed Real Estate Note Business.

Remember, you could earn thousands and thousands of dollars every time you transact a note deal. I've even seen my top students earn $5,000, $50,000 and more on their very first deal! Just follow my simple step-by-step program to establish a strong foundation for your business, and to change your financial future for forever. Just promise me that you will stay excited long enough to close your first deal. I know once you've done your first deal you'll never want to do anything else.

Again, I wish you great success in the best business in the world. If you have any questions, please let us know. My staff and I are here to help and we welcome your emails.

Happy hunting and best wishes for your business.

Warmly,

Russ Dalbey
Founder, *Dalbey Education*

The Real Estate Secret Success Stories

The money making success stories listed below have all followed the information in this book, applied it, worked at it, and made money. Keep in mind thousands and thousands of people have bought my system and most of them never report back to me. So I have no way of knowing the true average of "everyone". But I know for a fact, of the money making student who actually get back to me, the average is $3,600 per closed real estate IOU/note transaction.

First Name	Last Initial	State	Sum of Amount
Abraham	K	New York	$6,325.00
Alfred	B	Florida	$7,425.98
Alfred	F	Nevada	$5,200.00
Ambrose	C	Wisconsin	$1,167.40
Andrew	D	California	$2,640.00
Angel	T	Canada	$1,000.00
Annette	D	Canada	$6,689.00
Arlene	M	New York	$70,422.00
Asher	G	Florida	$6,398.00
Barbara	G	Pennsylivina	$869,457.72
Barry	G	Colorado	$1,409.00
Ben	M	Virgina	$27,278.78
Bert	A	Nevada	$1,644.27
Bill	N	Georigia	$907.00
Bill	B	Texas	$4,083.00
Bob & Carron	W	Kentucky	$1,000.00
Bob	M	Florida	$500.00
Bob	O	Missouri	$750.00
Brad	W	Alabama	$2,500.00
Brad	S	California	$18,000.00
Brian	R	Washington	$3,725.00
Bruce	L	New York	$1,000.00
Bruce	P	Texas	$148,797.19
Bruce	W	Arizonia	$3,929.50
Bud & Beverly	S	Arizonia	$2,000.00
Buddy	K	Louisanna	$3,336.72
Carlton	N	Florida	$9,773.00

Catherine	C	Georgia	$15,744.73
Charla	S	California	$2,100.00
Charles	B	Louisanna	$1,480.00
Charles	F	Michigan	$5,521.45
Charlie	T	Tennessee	$1,343.34
Chris & Rebecca	M	Oklahoma	$375.00
Christine	B	Oklahoma	$4,871.10
Christine	B	New York	$1,500.00
Chuck & Ryan	A	West Virginia	$3,615.00
Chuck	L	California	$64,847.92
Chuck	R	Virgina	$9,149.56
Clive	P	Nevada	$600.00
Curtis	Z	California	$4,369.21
Dallas	B	Texas	$2,225.00
Dan	J	South Carlonia	$1,025.00
Dan	B	New York	$179,947.19
Daniel	R	Florida	$1,100.38
Darrell	S	Washington	$46,006.25
Darrie	D	New Jersey	$1,500.00
Darryl	L	Illinois	$12,420.47
Daryla	J	Texas	$7,075.96
Darlys	S	Michigan	$262,216.00
Dave	Z	Illinois	$1,957.50
David	B	North Carlonia	$1,000.00
David	G	Florida	$27,250.00
David	S	Florida	$29,654.19
Dennis	S	California	$19,757.66
Diallo	C	New York	$2,500.00
Diane	M	New York	$9,137.00
Diane	P	Texas	$1,800.00
Diane	S	California	$5,000.00
Dianne	H	Georgia	$8,875.10
Dobie	L	Michigan	$600.00
Don & Julie	F	Georgia	$6,327.15
Don	D	New York	$2,925.00

Don	D	California	$500.00
Don	H	Virgina	$1,500.00
Don	M	Georgia	$2,000.00
Donna	B	California	$2,800.00
Dr. J.D.	V	Missouri	$3,243.00
Duane	G	Idaho	$3,600.00
Ed	L	California	$5,150.00
Ed	M	Montana	$900.00
Eden	A	Oklahoma	$40,665.92
Edwin	B	California	$1,052.00
Eileen	S '	North Dakota	$3,000.00
El	B	Indiana	$20,500.00
Enrique	S	California	$11,510.00
Eric	B	Texas	$1,403.62
Evelyn	E	Texas	$1,000.00
Faye	B	Nevada	$7,334.50
Name witheld	by request	undisclosed	$41,316.64
Garland	J	Georgia	$165,327.81
Gary	C	California	$91,911.20
Gary	T	Florida	$1,000.00
Gene	L	Georgia	$250.00
Gerald	C	Washington	$4,575.00
Gilberto	E	Texas	$2,819.00
Glenn	M	Oklahoma	$3,550.00
Grace	S	South Carlonia	$625.00
Greg	B	Florida	$4,100.00
Helga	H	California	$1,470.00
Henry	S	California	$2,500.00
Holly	M	New Jersey	$1,000.00
Ilene	G	Michigan	$3,210.00
Ira	S	Florida	$2,482.20
Jack	R	Florida	$2,000.00
James	H	Mississippi	$4,000.00
James	K	Nevada	$8,800.00
Jan	T	Wisconsin	$6,000.00

JaNae	H	Oregon	$8,138.00
Janice & Al	A	Missouri	$1,100.00
Janice	S	California	$2,300.00
Jason	S	Arizonia	$4,975.00
Jeff	H	Calilfornia	$17,340.00
Jennifer	D	Texas	$46,607.42
Jerry	D	Pennsylivina	$8,000.00
Jerry	D	Pennsylivina	$13,500.00
Jim & Sue	S	Michigan	$500.00
Jim	B	Texas	$2,000.00
Jim	C	Canada	$1,750.58
Jim	G	Nevada	$4,722.25
Jim	J	Texas	$2,000.00
Jim	M	Kansas	$1,350.60
Jo	K	Mississippi	$500.00
Joe	P	Florida	$3,000.00
Joe	R	California	$1,000.00
John	B	Oklahoma	$2,101.00
John	B	Texas	$1,000.00
John	B	Kentucky	$3,807.00
John	C	California	$682.96
John	C	Maryland	$719.27
John	H	Texas	$2,000.00
Jorge	M	California	$1,300.00
Joy	S	California	$1,250.00
Juan	D	Ohio	$500.00
Judy	U	Illinois	$1,850.00
Julian	G	Georgia	$406.04
Kara & Kija	E	Texas	$6,315.00
Karen	G	Georgia	$2,975.00
Kate & Chris	C	Illinois	$6,980.00
Kathi	Y	Ohio	$1,000.00
Kathy	W	New York	$2,000.00
Kathy	B	Arizona	$633.26
Ken	M	Oklahoma	$3,000.00

Kent	H	Texas	$7,500.00
Kerry	C	Ohio	$850.00
Kris	T	New Mexico	$1,952.11
Kristine	C	Ohio	$1,575.09
Kymberly	M	Ohio	$60,750.00
Lance	K	Washington	$2,100.00
Larry	W	Idaho	$1,126.25
Leonard	S	Missouri	$1,825.00
Leonette	B	Arizona	$13,619.03
Lewis	D	Texas	$9,459.50
Lily	T	California	$3,620.05
Linda	C	Texas	$1,493.72
Lisa	A	Iowa	$1,500.00
Lois & Charles	S	Alabama	$2,925.00
Louie	H	Florida	$1,000.00
Luisa	F	New York	$3,000.00
Luke	J	Virgina	$3,387.81
Lynette	G	New Mexico	$2,798.38
Mae	S	Texas	$5,142.34
Mal	B	California	$3,360.00
Marie	D	Texas	$18,606.50
Marjorie	V	Colorado	$500.00
Mark	H	Illinois	$500.00
Mark	S	Wisconsin	$22,430.00
Mark	T	Illinois	$4,000.00
Marsha	B	Ohio	$134,573.07
Martin	S	Kansas	$1,843.00
Michael	D	Louisanna	$15,000.00
Michael	M	Florida	$8,079.00
Michael	W	California	$1,000.00
Mike & Betty	C	Iowa	$227,921.00
Mike	W	Oregon	$1,000.00
Monique	D	California	$500.00
Mujeeb	N	Kansas	$4,500.00
Neal	B	Arizonia	$1,500.00

Nelson	M	Florida	$1,224.66
Nick	A	New York	$5,000.00
Nolan	P	Tennessee	$4,400.00
Nora	B	Michigan	$2,000.00
Norman	B	New Hampshire	$501.77
Norman	P	Washington	$5,177.34
Pam	F	California	$1,500.00
Pam	M	California	$1,500.00
Pamela	S	Oklahoma	$25,801.98
Pat	A	Colorado	$500.00
Patricia	G	Florida	$5,345.44
Patrick	W	Indiana	$1,381.50
Patty	M	Florida	$8,700.69
Paul	A	Florida	$59,359.53
Paul	F	Colorado	$21,200.00
Paul	H	West Virginia	$1,691.70
Paul	R	California	$2,500.00
Paul	S	Colorado	$2,289.00
Paul	S	Michigan	$5,368.34
Perry	D	California	$6,100.00
Philip	D	Georgia	$4,500.00
Phillip	L	Texas	$11,226.01
Priscella	O	California	$25,000.00
Randy and Tara	C	Colorado	$5,000.00
Randy	C	California	$5,000.00
Randy	P	Arizonia	$1,000.00
Regina	C	California	$2,000.00
Rena & Reginald	H	New York	$11,382.50
Rhonda	J	Missouri	$3,033.51
Rick & Betty Jo	K	Florida	$26,517.20
Rick	A	Texas	$500.00
Rick	T	Mississippi	$2,000.00
Rivkah	P	Texas	$500.00
Robert	H	Georgia	$3,842.00
Robert	M	California	$3,500.00

Robert	O	Colorado	$475.00
Rocky	S	California	$5,250.00
Roger	C	Arizona	$2,300.00
Ron	A	California	$1,500.00
Ron	L	Hawaii	$1,500.00
Ronald	D	Texas	$5,140.00
Royce	B	Texas	$53,859.55
Roz	V	California	$6,200.00
Russ	K	Ohio	$2,000.00
Russ	R	Colorado	$1,000.00
Ryan	A	North Carlonia	$5,000.00
Sandra	E	California	$1,500.00
Scot	A	California	$63,352.06
Sharon	L	Texas	$1,100.00
Sharon	S	Colorado	$11,052.96
Shawn	C	Nebraska	$7,070.17
Sheila	W	Wyoming	$7,500.00
Shirley	G	Alabama	$10,058.26
Simon	G	Washington	$882.50
Simon	M	Virgina	$4,000.00
Simon	S	Georgia	$300.00
Sonya	E	New Hampshire	$20,466.20
Sophia	J	Maryland	$193,672.29
Sterling	S	Oklahoma	$17,298.74
Steve	B	South Carlonia	$1,000.00
Steve	W	Virgina	$5,350.00
Steven	C	Colorado	$11,000.00
Stoney	B	Montana	$24,200.00
Sue	S	Arizona	$3,948.61
Sue	V	Indiana	$1,000.00
Susan	C	Oregon	$964.02
Susanne	J	Oregon	$7,849.00
Susie	S	Arkansas	$13,819.02
Suzanne	M	Colorado	$5,000.00
Tammy	P	North Carlonia	$3,129.22

Tanisha	M	Georgia	**$6,080.00**
Teresa	E	Colorado	**$1,000.00**
Theresa	R	Wisconsin	**$1,000.00**
Thomas	C	New Jersey	**$5,175.00**
Tim	K	Wisconsin	**$500.00**
Tim	M	Florida	**$1,000.00**
Tim	P	Michigan	**$3,400.00**
Tim	W	Texas	**$1,306.37**
Toby	J	Georgia	**$2,665.00**
Tom	F	Virgina	**$4,000.00**
Tom	K	Ohio	**$18,772.00**
Tom	M	Florida	**$2,500.00**
Toni	M	Connecticut	**$2,118.50**
Tyler	B	Alabama	**$1,741.28**
Tyler	D	Colorado	**$19,975.00**
Valetta	W	Oklahoma	**$1,706.94**
Velentina	S	California	**$10,000.00**
Vera	M	California	**$1,000.00**
Wayne	B	Idaho	**$7,600.00**
Wendi	J	Utah	**$1,900.00**
Will	M	Wyoming	**$2,500.00**
William	S	Nevada	**$5,000.00**
Total			**$4,001,732.70**

✚

		$
Your Name	**Your State**	**Your Profit**

GRAND TOTAL	$

LET ME HEAR ABOUT YOUR SUCCESS!

- Ross

Glossary

Accrued Interest:

The interest that has accumulated on a loan since the last interest payment up to, but not including, the settlement date.

Add-On Interest:

A procedure in which the interest payable during the term of the loan is added to the principal of the loan. The borrower signs a note promising to repay principal plus interest, although only the principal is initially disbursed to the borrower.

Adjustable Rate Mortgage (ARM):

A real estate loan wherein the interest rate paid on the remaining balance can go up or down at certain intervals specified in the loan. The interest rate paid is based on a specific index such as the rate paid by the government on Treasury Bills.

All-Inclusive Deed of Trust:

A form of deed of trust that, in addition to any other amounts actually financed includes the amounts of any prior deeds of trust. Also see "Wraparound Mortgage."

Amendment Of A Note:

The process of changing any existing terms of a note without actually writing a new note.

Amortized Loan:

A financing option in which payments over time cover principal and interest so the loan will be repaid in full at the end of the amortization period.

Annual Percentage Rate (APR):

A standard measure of how much interest an outstanding balance will cost you as a fee for the credit extended expressed as an annual percentage. Commonly applied on revolving credit accounts. From the point of view of the debtor (credit recipient), the lower the APR, the better.

Arrears:

The state of a debt that remains unpaid following the date of maturity. The term is commonly used in connection with mortgages, installment payments, such as is the case with notes, and other loans payments that are due on specified dates.

Assignee:

An individual to whom a title, claim, property, contract or right has been transferred.

Assignor:

The person transferring a title, claim, property, contract or right to a new owner.

Balloon Payment:

A large payment on a loan, usually due at the end of the payment schedule. There can also be partial balloon payments during the note term.

Bankruptcy:

A proceeding in a federal court that allows a person who is unable to repay outstanding debts to reorganize or discharge credit or debt obligations. A homeowner may delay foreclosure proceedings by filing for bankruptcy.

Beneficiary:

Person or entity (usually a lender) entitled to receive funds. The beneficiary receives these funds (payments) from the trustor.

Boiler Plate:

Slang for standardized legal language or template format writing often used in loan forms, real estate closings, and legal contracts.

Buy Down:

In order to reduce the interest and payments on a loan for the buyer, the property seller may pay the lender some money up front to "buy down" the interest and payments for a certain period of time. For example, if the seller buys down 3% of a 30-year loan at 14% interest, the buyer of the property only pays 11% interest for the first 2 years.

Buyer:

The person who purchases the real estate note you find.

Carry Paper:

Slang for creating and holding a note or loan. For example, the seller carried $20,000 in paper to facilitate the sale of his property.

Certified Public Accountant (CPA):

Provide legal and financial advice regarding the buying and selling of properties. A CPA who specializes in real estate can provide accounting considerations related to the development, ownership and operation of real estate assets. In addition, they can prepare financial statement considerations for real estate businesses and provide guidance on audit planning and performance.

Clear Title:

A property title that is free from liens, leases or other types of encumbrances.

Closing:

Completion of a transaction, including details like preparation and recording of legal documents, procurement of applicable insurance coverage, and transfer of funds.

Closing Costs:

The various fees and charges involved in closing a property transaction. These could include mortgage fees, title insurance and appraisal and inspection fees.

Collateral:

Property pledged as security for payment on an obligation.

Collection Service:

A neutral third party, other than the borrower or lender. The collection agency or collection service collects the payments due on a note and forwards the proceeds to the proper recipients.

Compound Interest:

Interest which is calculated not only on the initial principal, but also the accumulated interest. Compound interest differs from simple interest in that it is interest that has accrued interest. This is also know as "compounding."

Condominium:

A building or complex in which units of property can be individually owned. Each owner shares partial ownership of common areas with other owners in the building and usually pays a fee to a board or association that manages the building operation.

Contract for Deed:

A form of security instrument and debt contract wherein the owner of the property gives the buyer legal title only after the obligation has been paid in full. See "Land Contract."

Contractor:

A person or business which provides goods or services to another person or business under terms specified in a contract. Unlike an employee, a contractor does not regularly work for any business.

Conveyance:

The transfer of a property title from one entity to another (entity referring to an individual or a legal entity such as a corporation).

Courthouse:

Place where deeds and real estate paper are recorded. See also Recorder's Office and Register of Deeds.

Credit Report:

Independent sources compile information about an individual borrower, such as their credit history, payment history, account and loan information, credit inquiries, public record and collection items. Credit reports are listed with the three credit bureaus – Experian, TransUnion, and Equifax – and are used by lenders to determine a potential borrower's credit worthiness.

Creditor:

An individual or entity (such as a bank) that extends credit, in return for interest, to borrowers.

Current:

Term used to describe a loan on which the payments are up to date.

Current Principal Balance:

The balance currently owed on a note, which may be smaller or larger than the original principal balance.

Debt:

An amount owed to an individual or entity for funds borrowed. Debt can be represented by a loan, note, bond, mortgage or other form stating repayment terms and, if applicable, interest requirements. These different forms all imply intent to pay back an amount owed by a specific date, which is set forth in the repayment terms.

Debtor:

An individual or entity who owes money to an individual or entity (usually a bank). Debtors are bound to the terms of their borrowing agreement. If a debtor defaults on payments, their assets can also become liable for the debt.

Debt Service:

The monthly payments required to keep the loans on a property current.

Deed of Trust:

Some states refer to mortgage documents as a Deed of Trust, also referred to as a "Trust Deed," "Mortgage Deed" and "Security Deed." The Deed of Trust transfers the title of the property to a trustee (often a title company) who holds it as a security for a loan. When the loan is paid off, the title is transferred to the borrower. The trustee will not become involved in the arrangement unless the borrower defaults on the loan. At that point, the trustee can sell the property and pay the lender from the proceeds. Also see "Trust Deed."

Default:

Failure to make required debt payments on a timely basis or to comply with the terms and conditions of the borrowing agreement.

Delinquent:

Payments that are past due and not paid at the scheduled time.

Discount:

A purchase price less than the remaining principal balance of a note.

Discounted Paper:

Real estate notes bought or sold at a price less than the principal balance.

Discounting:

The practice of adjusting the price of a note to compensate for other factors such as term, payments, interest rate, security, and needs of the seller. The discount raises the yield or return to the buyer.

Discount Points:

A point is one percent of the principal amount. For example, a note that has a face interest rate of 9% is discounted 3 points when purchased at a yield of 12%.

Double Escrow:

Two separate, but related escrows or closings, each contingent or dependent on the other. For example, you are buying a note and reselling it immediately for profit. The buy and resale of the note closings are contingent on each other and close at the same time (within 72 hours).

Down Payment:

A lump sum cash payment paid by a property buyer when he or she purchases a property. The buyer typically takes out a loan for the balance remaining, and pays it off in monthly installments over time.

Due-on-Sale Clause:

A provision in a mortgage contract that requires that the mortgage be repaid in full if the borrower sells the mortgaged property before the loan is paid off.

Effective Interest Rate:
The overall yield earned on an investment, taking into account the discount, all existing loan terms and the effects of compounding.

Equity:
The amount left over after subtracting the loans, or any other claims, on the property from the market value of the property.

Equity Cushion:
The margin of safety over and above a specific loan on a property. A $100,000 property with $65,000 in loans would have a $35,000 equity cushion to protect the loans; the equity a lender may require before making a loan.

Escalation:
Rising loan payments over time.

Escrow:
A neutral third party that receives the instruments, contracts, documents and funds in a transaction as needed from both a buyer and a seller. This third party sees that specific terms and conditions are met before releasing money, instruments and/or property to their respective participants.

Escrow Agent:
The designated third party that gathers the necessary documents, signatures, sets a date for closing on a property transaction and handles the transfer of funds and title. Both the buyer and the seller must agree on using this third party by forming a contractual agreement. State law dictates who the third party can be, such as an escrow company, attorney, title company or other approved parties.

Escrow Instructions:
Instructions for a neutral third party (escrow agent) that are signed by both the buyer and seller that must be carried out before a transaction may take place.

Execution:
The legal signing of a document. In order to record an instrument, a Notary Public must witness its execution.

Existing Financing:

The financing on a property before making any changes. Example: When looking for a property to buy, you are first interested in the existing financing. See also Proposed Financing.

Extension Agreement:

A written agreement giving a debtor more time to pay on an obligation.

Face Value:

The original principal balance appearing on the note. Be sure to check the current principal balance of a seasoned note because it may be drastically different than the face value.

Finding:

The act of referring a note to a buyer and making quick cash profits.

Financial Calculator:

A specific type of calculator designed for dealing with calculations involving money, loans, payments, and time. An example of a financial calculator is the Hewlett Packard HP10BII.

First Loan:

Usually refers to a mortgage, trust deed or promissory note that has first claim in the event of a default.

Foreclosure:

A procedure by which a property being used as security for a loan is sold to pay money owed to the lender as a result of a default in payments or terms.

Free and Clear:

Property that has no liens, especially voluntary liens (mortgages).

Fully Amortized:

A loan whose payments include both interest and principal and will be paid in full during its term with no balloon payment.

Future Value:

The value of a dollar or loan amount at a designated future date.

Green Note:
   A term used to describe notes that do not meet buyers desired seasoning standards. Generally speaking, most buyers prefer to see at least 6-12 months of seasoning.

Hard Money:
   Cash loaned for the purchase of property from a private party. Usually these loans have short terms with high interest rates.

Holder:
   The current owner of a promissory note.

Imputed Interest:
   When the interest rate on a mortgage is below a certain rate determined by the IRS, the IRS imputes or charges the property seller tax on the higher rate of interest. For more detailed information, please consult your tax advisor.

Imputed Principal:
   When the buyer of the property gets an interest rate below a certain rate specified by the IRS, the IRS may impute or declare that the actual property sales price was lower than stated in the purchase contract. For more detailed information, please consult your tax advisor.

Installment:
   One of a series of payments on a note.

Installment Note:
   A note that is payable in individual payments called installments.

Instrument:
   The legal document used as evidence of debt, title, lien, etc.

Interest (I/YR):
   A charge (usually monthly) for borrowing money. Also see "Add-On Interest," "Compound Interest" and "Simple Interest."

Interest Extra:
   Loan payment terms wherein the payment goes to principal and not to interest.

Interest Included:

Loan payment terms wherein the payment goes to interest first and any surplus goes to reducing the principal.

Interest Only:

Loan payment terms wherein the payment is exactly equal to the monthly interest, not more and not less.

Intermediate-Term Loan:

Most intermediate-term loans are set between 1-3 years and typically carry fixed interest rates and monthly repayment schedules.

Internal Revenue Service (IRS):

Division of the Department of the Treasury responsible for collecting taxes.

Investment to Value (ITV):

The percentage ratio between the purchase cost of a note and the value of a property.

Junior Lien:

A loan recorded at a later date than the senior loans. The security instrument recorded next after the first loan would be a second. It is junior to the first.

Land Contract:

A security instrument wherein the seller (Vendor) gives the buyer (Vendee) possession of the property, but retains legal title (the deed) as security for a loan until specific payment has been made. The buyer of the property gets "equitable title" and the right to use and enjoy the property and tax benefits prior to actually receiving the deed.

Late Charges:

Fees or penalties owed to a lender when payments are late, as stated in the terms of the loan.

Lease Option to Buy:

A lease under which the lessee (renter) has the option to purchase the property.

Level Payments:
Loan payment terms wherein payments stay the same each period, neither increasing nor decreasing with time.

Liabilities:
An obligation that legally binds an individual or company to settle a debt. When one is liable for a debt, they are responsible for paying the debt.

Lien:
Any claim against a property, including mortgages, unpaid taxes, repair bills or other unpaid charges. Prospective property buyers conduct a title search to determine whether any liens against the property exist. A lien must be filed or recorded with the local county government to be attached to a property title. Recorded loans are liens.

Line of Credit (LOC):
The ability to borrow money repeatedly, up to a set credit dollar limit, without having to re-apply with each use. A line of credit or "credit line" can be either "secured" or "unsecured" – secured means that the credit is made against an item of real value that the borrower has a stake in. An unsecured credit line – also referred to as a "signature loan" – grants borrowing ability without having to pledge specific collateral – usually real estate or vehicle equity – in order to obtain this credit. Having a line of credit can be invaluable for businesses that have seasonal fluctuations in revenue or irregular income patterns. Also see "Signature Loan."

Liquidate:
To sell an investment (property) and turn that asset into cash. When a company is going out of business they will liquidate (sell) all of their assets to pay outstanding debts or distribute it to their shareholders.

Loan:
The granting of the use of money or equity in return for payment. The loan includes the right of one party to collect from another according to the loan agreement or note. There are existing loans (already there) and new loans (ones just being created).

Loan Balance:
   The amount needed to pay off a loan.

Loan to Value Ratio (LTV):
   The percentage ratio between the amount of the total loans on a property and the property value.

Loan Value:
   The maximum for a loan that most lenders would lend on a property. Assuming an 80% loan to value ratio, the Loan Value on a $100,000 property would be $80,000.

Long-Term:
   Most long-term loans are set between 3-10 years though some can go as long as 20-30 years. They typically carry fixed interest rates, monthly or quarterly repayment schedules and include a set maturity date.

Maker:
   The person who signs a note, agreeing to pay it.

Marketable:
   A note is marketable when there are a large number of potential buyers for it, based on note size, security, yield, and terms.

Market Value:
   The price buyers would pay and sellers would accept for a note.

Maturity:
   The time when an obligation of debt becomes due and must be paid in full.

Multiple Listing Service (MLS):
   A database of real estate listings for sale. Multiple Listing Service (MLS) is commonly used by real estate agents, real estate brokers and Realtors® to research what properties are for sale. Each property listed on the MLS is assigned an eight-digit ID number.

Moratorium:
　　Suspension of foreclosure proceedings for a specific period of time. Often times this is used by the lender to determine a modified loan solution.

Mortgage:
　　A security instrument, which pledges a property to insure payment of a note. In case of default, property can go into foreclosure.

Mortgage Broker:
　　A party who joins borrowers and lenders for loan creation, earning a placement fee.

Mortgage Lien:
　　A legal claim against a mortgaged property, which must be paid when the property is sold.

Mortgagee:
　　The lender or person collecting payments on a mortgage.

Mortgage Release:
　　Notice of debt satisfaction by the lender when the loan has been paid in full.

Mortgagor:
　　The borrower making monthly payments on a mortgage loan to the mortgagee.

Negative Amortization:
　　A loan structured with payments below accruing interest, ultimately creating a higher principal balance than initially borrowed.

Negative Cash Flow:
　　When the outflow of money is greater than the amount coming in.

Negotiable Instrument:
　　A document such as a personal check or note. It must meet certain legal requirements in order to be transferred (negotiated) from one holder to another.

Nominal Interest Rate:

The face interest rate on a loan. Nominal interest rates are not adjusted for inflation.

Notary Public:

An individual with legal authorization to authenticate signatures and/or the execution of instruments and documents.

Note:

A written promise to pay, with all the terms and conditions of the obligation, signed and in proper legal format. Also referred to as a "Promissory Note." A note can be secured or unsecured. Also see "Secured Loan" and "Unsecured Loan."

Note Finder:

Someone who collects and organizes information about a seller financed real estate note and presents it to a buyer, usually for a profit or "finders fee." Note finders are not agents, nor do they work on the note holder's or note buyer's behalf.

Note Holder:

An individual currently in ownership and possession of a note who is entitled to collect payments. The holder might not be the original beneficiary as many notes are assumable.

Note Owner:

See Note Holder.

Note Payment Book (Record):

A simple record of all payments made on a note showing how much was paid each payment. It breaks each payment down to principal and interest, and shows the current principal balance.

No Money Down:

Acquiring property with no cash out of pocket. This does not mean that the seller and/or real estate agent did not receive cash. Cash can come from more places than just the buyer.

Notice of Default (NOD):

Recorded at the county recorder's office and starts the foreclosure process. The NOD officially notifies the property owner of the lender's foreclosure intentions. The NOD also starts the reinstatement period in which the property owner has the opportunity to bring the loan current. States that conduct non-judicial foreclosures require an NOD be filed.

Notice of Sale (NOS):

Initiates the second stage of foreclosure and will be issued to the property owner if the loan is not brought current during the right to cure period of the NOD. The NOS will physically be attached to the property and listed in local newspapers with a set future date of sale.

Novation:

Rewriting an old document and replacing it with the new one.

Obligee:

The person to whom payments are owed according to the terms of a note.

Obligor:

The person obligated to make the payments on a note.

Offset Statement:

A written statement by a lender or borrower concerning the current status of a loan. It includes the current principal balance, whether payments are current or not, and terms and conditions of the loan.

Option:

The right to buy something for a stated price and terms within a certain time period. Something must be paid for this right. This is called option consideration. The option will either be exercised (used) or abandoned (not used).

Optionee:

The person who has the right to buy under an option.

Optionor:

The person who has agreed to sell property under an option.

Original Principal Balance:

The principal owed on a note the day it started. This is contrasted to the current principal balance, which may be different. Also see "Face Value."

Origination:

The creation of something, in this case a note and security instrument.

"Or More" Clause:

A clause in a note stating that the monthly payments are to be a specified amount of dollars "Or More."

Or Order:

A clause in a note, such as "Pay to Joe Jones or order." The "or order" would be an assignee or future owner of the note.

Owner:

The person having title to something such as a property or a note.

Owner Occupied:

A property in which the owner lives.

Paper:

A promissory note secured by real estate.

Partial Amortization:

Loan payments that cover principal and interest for a certain period of time and at a predetermined date a balloon payment of the remaining balance is due.

Payee:

The person to whom payments are due.

Payment (PMT):

The amount of money paid in each installment on a note or loan.

Payment Book:

See Note Payment Book.

Payment Schedule:

Defines how much each payment is and when each payment is due.

Payor:

   The person obligated to make the payments on a note. Also referred to as the "Mortgagor" with a mortgage contract or a "Trustor" with a trust deed.

Percentage:

   A fraction expressed in one-hundredths. This is used for interest rates, for example 0.09 is 9%. 9% simple interest on $100,000 is $9,000 per year.

Personal Note:

   An unsecured note. The maker has personal liability on a personal note.

PITI:

   Principal, Interest, Taxes and Insurance. On an amortized loan that has an impound or escrow account for taxes and insurance, the monthly payment consists of Principal, Interest, Taxes and Insurance (PITI).

Points:

   A point is 1% of the principal. See also Discount Points.

Positive Cash Flow:

   When the inflow of money is greater than that going out.

Prepayment:

   Paying of a loan, either in part or in full, before the maturity date (due date).

Prepayment Clause:

   A provision in a promissory note that sets any penalties that result if the borrower repays the balance of the note ahead of schedule.

Present Value:

   The current worth or dollar amount of payments that are to be collected in the future.

Principal:

   The amount of money that is borrowed through a loan or note.

Principal Balance:

The remaining amount of a loan or note. Depending on the terms of the loan, this may be more or less than the original face amount of the note.

Private Party Financing:

Phrase used to describe a note or loan carried by an individual person.

Promissory Note:

A legal written promise to pay a certain amount according to its terms and conditions.

Property Owner:

The person who owns the property which is the security for a note. The property owner is usually the one who owes and pays on the note.

Proposed Financing:

How loan terms are intended to look after the closing of a current transaction.

Protective Equity:

Phrase used to describe the imaginary "cushion" created by the difference between the loan on a property and the current property value. For example, a property valued at $100,000 with $65,000 in loans against it would have $35,000 of protective equity.

Purchase Money:

Money that is loaned for the purchase of real property. This can be in the form of seller carry back financing or a new bank loan. It is contrasted to Refinance Money or Hard Money. In certain cases it may carry no personal liability and may not be subject to deficiency judgments.

Rate of Return:

The total amount earned or lost on a particular investment proportional to the initial amount invested. Positive rate of return is often referred to as a yield or interest rate.

Real Estate Agent:

A person who is state licensed to negotiate and arrange real estate sales but works for a real estate broker or brokerage agency.

Real Estate Attorney:

An attorney who specializes in all aspects of property law, including: property disputes, commercial and residential leasing issues, purchase or sale of property, setting or renegotiating real estate contracts or note terms, real estate agent or broker disputes or issues, land and zoning issues, etc.

Real Estate Broker:

A person or business entity that is state licensed to sponsor real estate agents and sell real estate for a fee. It is the broker that has ultimate responsibility for the actions and practices of the agents that work for them.

Real Estate Paper:

Notes secured by real estate and held by private parties; not banks, professional loan finders, or real estate agents in the business of dealing with notes for profit. Real estate paper can include: Mortgages, Deeds of Trust, Security Deeds, and Land Contracts.

Recast:

To adjust the terms of an existing loan or mortgage that is facing default. Examples of this may include extending the life or interest rate of the loan or mortgage to ensure the borrower can make the payments. Some loans or mortgages have a recast set to take place at a designated time, such as 5 years after the first payment, but this would be included in the initial terms.

Reconveyance:

The transferring of a title back to its previous owner. When a trust deed is used to secure payment of a loan or a mortgage is paid off, the trustee reconveys the title back to the property owner and releases the lien from the property.

Recordation:

The formal recording (filing) of a legal document such as a security instrument. Recordation with the County Recorder's Office or other appropriate governmental office serves constructive notice to the world that the document exists.

Recorder's Office:

The local governmental agency responsible for maintaining official records of documents filed therein, such as deeds and security instruments (real estate paper). Also referred to as the "county courthouse" or "Register of Deeds."

Recourse:

When signing (endorsing) a note from one party to another, you do so either with or without recourse. With recourse means that you still have contingent liability to the buyer of the note. In the event the maker doesn't pay as promised, you have to pay. Also see "Without Recourse."

Redemption:

In a foreclosure situation, redemption is the right to pay off the loan in full (plus foreclosure fees) and either stop the foreclosure while in progress or get the property back after it has been sold. Also see "Redemption Period."

Redemption Period:

The period of time during a foreclosure when the debtor has the right to make payment in full and stop the proceedings. Also a period after the property has been sold through foreclosure in which the foreclosed owner can pay the loan amount plus applicable charges and get the property back. This varies according to state law.

Refinance:

Paying off an existing loan on a property through the creation of a new or renegotiated contract (loan).

Register of Deeds:

See Recorder's Office, Courthouse.

Reinstatement:

In the beginning of a foreclosure, the debtor has the right to catch up on payments and additional foreclosure fees, ultimately bringing the loan current. If the payer does so, the original terms of the contract will remain in place.

Reinstatement Period:

The time period specified by local law, in which the debtor has the right to catch up on payments and additional foreclosure fees, ultimately bringing the loan current.

Release of Liability:

Appropriate documentation from a lender, releasing the payor of debt and any liens associated with it.

Release of Mortgage:

A written instrument releasing a mortgage lien from a property. Also called a Certificate of Discharge.

Renegotiate:

To change the terms and conditions of an existing loan by mutual agreement of the lender and payor. Either party can initiate a renegotiation.

Request for Reconveyance:

Appropriate documentation from the beneficiary of a trust deed, to the trustee, stating the terms and conditions of the initial obligations have been met. Usually, this written instrument is official proof of debt satisfaction from the lender. Also see "Reconveyance."

Reverse Polish Notation (RPN):

A form of calculator logic or programming in which the number is entered before the operation (plus, minus, times, divided by). The Hewlett Packard HP12c uses RPN.

Risk:

A determination of how safe or dangerous a specific investment is.

Rollover Note:

A relatively short-term (5 years or less) note that renews at the end of each term. This renewal usually comes with a different set of loan terms (interest rate, length, and payment amount).

Satisfaction of Mortgage:

A document signed by the lending party that indicates that the terms of repayment have been completed and releases the payor from liability on a mortgage.

Seasoned Note:

A note becomes "seasoned" after the payor makes consistent payments to the note holder. Most agree twelve (12) months of payments should be made in order for a note to be "seasoned." However, some note buyers consider a note with six (6) months of payments to be a "seasoned" note. If the note is not "seasoned" to the buyer's standards, it is considered to be a "green note."

Second Position Lien:

The lien immediately junior to the first position lien, it is subordinate to claims made by those liens that were recorded prior.

Secured Loan:

A loan (note), which has specific collateral pledged to secure its payment. In the event payment is not made, the collateral can be reclaimed by the lender. In most cases it will be sold to provide funds to pay for the remaining balance on the note.

Security Deed:

See Deed of Trust.

Security Instrument:

The official legal document which, when properly recorded, places a lien on the property to secure the payment on a note. The most common security instruments are mortgages and trust deeds. Should the payor default on this obligation, this document allows the property to be sold.

Seller Carry-Back Financing:

The seller of a property creates a note secured by the property as part of the payment for sale. Also see "Owner Financing."

Seniority:

The order of repayment in cases of default – senior debts must be repaid prior to those in the junior positions. Because of this, senior liens are more secure than junior liens. In most cases, seniority is determined by the order in which documents are recorded. The first lien recorded is the "First," the next is the "Second," etc.

Senior Lien:

A lien recorded before others. A lien can be senior to some and junior to others. For example, a second loan is a senior to a third loan but junior to a first loan.

Short-Term Loan:

A note that has a repayment period of 1 year or less at origination or remaining term.

Signature Loan:

A loan where no collateral has been pledged. Signature loans are granted based on the customer's promise to repay and the signing of an agreement specifying repayment terms. Evidence of past history of being able to meet similar payment demands is necessary for an individual or company to obtain a signature loan. Also referred to as an "unsecured line of credit" or an "unsecured personal loan," signature loans typically have higher interest rates than secured loans.

Simple Interest:

Interest is calculated on the original principal only and accumulated interest from prior periods is not compounded into following periods.

Simultaneous Closing:

A term referring to the purchase and sale of real estate property or the creation and sale of a lien at the same time (or sometimes within a few days of each other).

Stop Date:

The date of the last payment on a note. It may be fully amortized or there may be a balloon payment. Also referred to as "Call Date."

Straight Note:

A loan with periodic payments of interest-only and then the principal sum is due in one lump sum upon maturity.

Subject To Clause:

Purchasing a property "subject to" an existing lien on the property with the purchaser making payments on the previous owner's loan. Though the original owner is still legally bound to pay his original loan, an additional agreement is signed between the home buyer and the seller indicating that the buyer is responsible for making payments to the seller on that existing loan.

Success Team:

The team of professionals you work with to complete your real estate and note deals. Can include real estate attorneys, real estate agents or brokers, CPAs, appraisers, contractors, or any other professional resource you utilize to bring in to find and complete your deals.

Term:

The length of time a loan runs. For example a note can have a 360 month (30 year) "term."

Terms:

The main features of a loan: principal amount, interest rate, payment schedule, and due date.

Trust Deed or Deed of Trust:

A deed given by the borrower to a trustee to be held pending fulfillment of an obligation. This is the security instrument, which pledges the property to insure payment on the note.

Trustee:

One who holds property in trust for another to secure the performance of an obligation. An example of a trustee would be a title company or attorney.

Trustor:

The person who conveys property in trust. One who deeds his property to a trustee to be held as security until he has performed under the terms of a deed of trust.

Truth in Lending Laws:

Legislation that pertains to fair dealing and full disclosure in making new loans. It does not apply to the sale of existing notes.

Uneven Payments:

If the payments of a loan vary from time to time, they are said to be "uneven" payments. Example: $100/month the first year, then $200/month the second year, and then $300/month thereafter.

Unsecured Loan:

An unsecured note or personal note. It is secured only by the maker's written promise to pay. No specific security has been pledged to back up the promise to pay.

Unsecured Note:

See Unsecured Loan.

Usury:

The illegal act of charging very high interest rates on loans. There are "usury" laws, which specify the maximum rate private parties can charge on loans. Above that rate, it is "usury" and the loan would be "usurious." There is absolutely no limit as to how much yield a person can get when they buy a promissory note at discount, however.

Value:

What one party is willing to pay for something. There are as many values for something as there are parties considering owning it. When there is widespread agreement of value, we have a market value (generally agreed-upon price such as the price of gasoline). On the other hand, notes have a less well-defined market. Therefore, negotiation has a large part in determining value or price.

Warranty Deed:

A type of deed where the seller guarantees that he or she holds clear title to a piece of real estate and has a right to sell it to you. The guarantee is not limited to the time the seller owned the property – it extends back to the property's origins.

Without Recourse:

The way of endorsing a note to an assignee. This protects the assignor from any further liability on the sale, even in the event the Maker fails to pay on the note. This is the way to sell a note to protect yourself. See also Recourse.

Wrap-Around Contract:

A Land Contract that wraps around earlier existing financing. See Wrap-Around Mortgage.

Wrap-Around Mortgage:

A larger Mortgage that "wraps around' a smaller senior lien. The debtor pays to the holder of the "Wrap-Around" and the holder of the "Wrap" pays on the included senior lien.

Writ of Execution:

A court order giving permission to seize a debtor's property to satisfy a debt.

Yield:

A percentage rate that measures the cash returns or income earned on a specific investment.

Index

A

B

C

N

O

P